D1709633

DESIGN OF ENCLOSED SPACES

DESIGN OF ENCLOSED SPACES

PIERA SCURI

CHAPMAN & HALL

I(T)P An International Thomson Publishing Company

New York • Albany • Bonn • Boston • Cincinnati • Detriot • London • Madrid • Melbourne • Mexico City
Pacific Grove • Paris • San Francisco • Singapore • Tokyo • Toronto • Washington

Cover photo courtesy of: IGuzzini Illuminazione
Cover design: Trudi Gershenov

Copyright © 1995
By Chapman & Hall
A division of International Thomson Publishing Inc.
I(T)P The ITP logo is a trademark under license

Printed in the United States of America

For more information, contact:

Chapman & Hall
One Penn Plaza
New York, NY 10119

International Thomson Publishing
Berkshire House 168-173
High Holborn
London WC1V 7AA
England

Thomas Nelson Australia
102 Dodds Street
South Melbourne, 3205
Victoria, Australia

Nelson Canada
1120 Birchmount Road
Scarborough, Ontario
Canada M1K 5G4

International Thomson Editores
Campos Eliseos 385, Piso 7
Col. Polanco
11560 Mexico D.F. Mexico

International Thomson Publishing Gmbh
Königwinterer Strasse 418
53228 Bonn
Germany

International Thomson Publishing Asia
221 Henderson Road #05-10
Henderson Building
Singapore 0315

International Thomson Publishing- Japan
Hirakawacho-cho Kyowa Building,3F
1-2-1 Hirakawacho-cho
Chiyoda-ku, 102 Tokyo
Japan

1 2 3 4 5 6 7 8 9 10 XXX 01 00 99 98 97 96 95

Library of Congress Catloging-in-Publication Data
Scuri, Piera.
    Design of enclosed spaces / Piera Scuri.
        p.   cm.
    Includes bibliographical references.
    ISBN 0-412-98961-1
    1. Interior architecture. 2. Personal space. 3. Space
(Architecture) I. Title.
    NA2850 . S39 1994   94-13396
    729 --dc20   CIP

British Library Cataloguing in Publication Data available

Please send your order for this or any other Chapman & Hall book to
Chapman & Hall, 29 West 35th Street, New York, NY 10001, Attn: Customer Service Department.
You many also call our Order Department at 1-212-244-3336 or fax you purchase order to 1-800-248-4724.

For a complete listing of Chapman & Hall's titles, send your request to
Chapman & Hall, Dept. BC, One Penn Plaza, New York, NY 10119.

CONTENTS

ACKNOWLEDGMENTS

This book is not the work of one person, and it is a pleasure to acknowledge here those who have been of help. We thank: Donatella Ravizza, who did the major work of gathering photographs; Dida Biggi for her beautiful pictures; Charles Poynton for providing such interesting ideas on color science; Douglas Skene, who helped shape this volume through his ideas; and Dr. Alessandro Meluzzi for his collobaration regarding "Light Therapy."

Thanks are owed to NASA, ESA, the Lighting Research Center of the Rensselaer Polytechnic Institute, Biblioteca Comunale di Milano, Biblioteca Trivulziana, Biblioteca d'Arte di Milano, Soprintendenza per i Beni Artistici e Storici di Mantova, Famiglia Malinverni, and IGuzzini Illuminazione.

NOTES TOWARD A PURPOSEFUL SENSE OF SPACE

A number of years ago, I conducted some research at the University of Rome into the relationship between architecture and psychiatry. The project generated an appalling quantity of papers, data, observations, and ideas, all of which were almost totally useless. Psychiatrists were at pains to stress the negative aspects of any new experiments in building and made a series of recommendations: Corridors should continue to be straight in order to allay the fears of disturbed people who imagine that a killer is lying in wait for them behind every bend; symmetrical designs were preferable because they lend a sense of security; anything uncertain, vague, or ambiguous was to be avoided in order not to incur states of worry and anguish. In the end, I proposed a pact with the psychiatrists taking part in the study: Either they cured the sick and rendered them capable of living in modern, dynamic, flowing spaces that stimulate the imagination, or we would be forced to design architectural corpses, buildings that were static, classicist, boring, and sepulchral.

In this study, Piera Scuri takes the opposite view to that of yesterday's university psychiatrists. For her, space is a protagonist, not a mere container; it is the manager and promoter of its contents, indicating and stimulating alternatives. She perceives space as an architectural language, a language that is receptive to countless stimuli, but endowed also with an independence that conditions, transforms, and censures anachronistic solutions.

My own study, entitled *Il linguaggio moderno dell'architettura - Guida ad un codice anticlassico,* is cited on several occasions in the present work. The reason for this is simple: Although the author and I proceed along paths that differ quite markedly from one another, where we do come together is in a shared inspiration, an inspiration that began as scientific and artistic, and later turned civil. Both paths lead to the conclusion that the repression of liberty precedes, follows, or accompanies the repression of architectural space.

Three points of controversy are:

The Design of Underground Environments.   Tombs or nightclubs? Renunciation of life or perverse hedonism? Or yet again, a perfidious political strategy like that of the catacombs of the third century AD, which ate away the ground upon which the shining, rhetorical, monumental imperial city was erected, ultimately causing its collapse.

Seeing by Touch.   Or rather, grasping, clutching at hollows, taking possession of the empty spaces, their depth, the lights and half-shadows. By such means, the "sensory starvation" of the remote past and that of the technological age are overcome.

The Symbolic Dimension.   The writer observes that it is "above all in relation to classical architecture" that this may be mentioned. All the more reason for discussing it very little, given the lack of faith inspired by an architecture that favors the messages of the underworld over its human obligations.

In these inquiries into spatial realities, I discern a danger in that tendency which wishes to order and normalize anomalous environments, to attenuate differences, shocks, traumas. Let us recall what has been written about "deconstructivist architecture": The ideal is no longer the academic ideal of the union, or balance, of universal and eternal values. Architects now know how to rejoice in their sense of "disquiet." They reject cubes, right angles, and symmetry, preferring disharmony, fragmentation, and mystery to harmony and unity. Dissonance is a basic characteristic of modern art, but it must become a reality in architectural space. Happiness is the aim, not escapism.

BRUNO ZEVI

DESIGN OF ENCLOSED SPACES

CHAPTER 1

ARTIFICIAL VERSUS NATURAL

Transformations

The castles and medieval villages of Central Italy, built on strategic hilltop sites, blend perfectly with the surrounding landscape in a balanced and harmonious relationship with the natural world. (Photo: Douglas Skene.)

The environments we live in have undergone profound and rapid change. Paradoxically, we have grown accustomed to these changes without even noticing them. Because phenomena regarding the environment are considered obvious or banal, both their analysis and their identification are made extremely difficult (here as elsewhere, it is useful to recall Whitehead's paradox whereby nothing is more mysterious than the obvious). Most of the changes that have come about have been in the physical conditions of the environment—particularly those of cities—and have affected the air, light, colors, materials, dimensions, noises, smells, and spatial conformations. It could be said, to borrow a technological term (no

accident, this), that these changes have affected above all the so-called soft structures of architecture (as opposed to the hard structures, i.e., the building/construction dimension). As an aspect of the environment, these soft structures have a considerable influence on our way of life.

In order to gain a better understanding of the relationship that is established between the human body and space, some researchers have distinguished several different analytical categories. Niels Prak for example, lists four: (1) the visual level (the space I see around me); (2) the conceptual level (the space I imagine when I close my eyes or enter another room); (3) the behavioral level (the spatial conformations that force me to move in a certain way: if there is a hole in the middle of the room, I will have to walk around it; (4) the physical level (if a window is opened and it is cold outside, the sensations I experience in that room will change, even though I continue to see it in the same way as before).[1] According to the terms of this classification, we shall be particularly concerned in this study with the physical level of the human-organism–space relationship. Its importance is such that it overshadows all other aspects, concerning as it does the very survival of the organism itself.

"Gallery of the Hotel de Villars," J.B. Leroux and N. Pineau, watercolor. (Courtesy of Istituto di Storia dell'Arte, Fondazione Cini, Venezia.)

Interiors

The spatial dimension that most conditions our way of life is the interior: Our perceptions and mental states are directly influenced by it (and yet in discussions about architecture, attention is usually focused on those aspects concerning construction and structure, or else the subject is tackled from an aesthetic point of view). This results in far greater consideration being given to the mental (conceptual-symbolic) approach, to the detriment of the physical (sensory-emotional) approach. Space reflects, by means of the transformations it undergoes, the characteristics of and the changes in the society that inhabits it. Interiors are especially revealing about the era that creates them (as Mario Praz puts it, the house is a mirror that reflects the personalities, desires, and fears of its inhabitants). And this is especially true of certain historical epochs. House interiors in the eighteenth century played much the same role as Gothic cathedrals in the Middle Ages: They were the "miroir moral" of the age. Confirming this thesis, Jean Starobinski states that the eighteenth century left its mark above all on the interior, and that this was no accident:

> It was above all on interior decoration that the 18th century left its mark, at least up to the generation of Boullée and the Ledoux which in fact introduced few innovations to the exterior forms of an architecture that displayed the elements of a classical language, skillfully remodelled and sweetened. The designers of friezes and fireplaces, the cabinet-makers, goldsmiths, tailors, hairdressers and cooks gave proof of an inexaustible inspiration in order to be able to satisfy such an

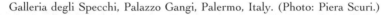

Galleria degli Specchi, Palazzo Gangi, Palermo, Italy. (Photo: Piera Scuri.)

Palladio's Villa Rotonda is a good example of architecture conceived on the basis of a strong relationship with the external world, in this case with the hills of the countryside around Vicenza. The villa's very shape seems to echo this relationship: Its central body seems almost to explode in an outward direction. Plan and vertical section of Villa Rotonda From Andrea Palladio, *I quattro libri dell'architettura,* Venice, Carampello, 1581. (Courtesy of Biblioteca Trivulziana, Castello Sforzesco, Milan.)

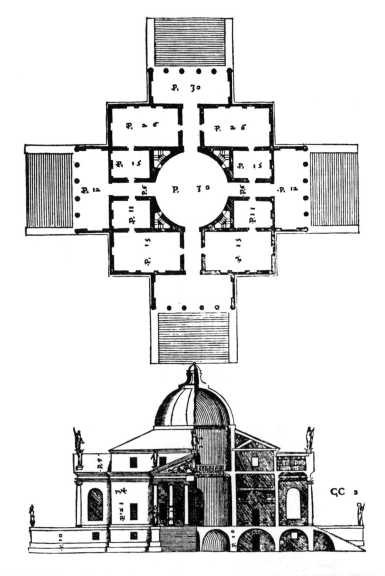

Villa Rotonda, circa 1570, Vicenza, Italy. Architect: Andrea Palladio. (Photo: Donatella Ravizza.)

artificially hedonistic way of life. In a world of ostentation, in which personal pleasure is valued more highly than future splendour, it was natural that greater importance be accorded those things which surrounded people more closely—clothes, furniture, jewels, trinkets and the decoration of the living spaces. And since taste was subordinate to the predominant criterion of individual pleasure, it demanded variety, surprise effects and continual change, so that one fashion rapidly followed the next. . . . Artifice was further accentuated by the fact that the growing bourgeoisie, in its rush to have access to the visible advantages, presumed to exhibit its victory by imitating the ways of the court.[2]

What, if we were to adopt Starobinski's approach, might we say about the environments that constitute our daily surroundings now (for theoretically, the environments discussed in the present text differ neither geographically nor culturally, whether they be American or European)? The role played by the apartment at the end of the eighteenth and beginning of the nineteenth century in Europe (and the cathedral in the Middle Ages) is now played by offices, shopping centers, amusement parks, and discotheques in the whole of the industrialized world. They are the new typologies of our era: environments built by us and that at the same time build us. And their effects on our organism are not limited to the psychological sphere; they also touch the physiological sphere. Although very high levels of artifice were reached in eighteenth and nineteenth century interiors, elements such as air

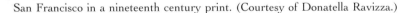

San Francisco in a nineteenth century print. (Courtesy of Donatella Ravizza.)

and light remained unchanged. Only in the present century did man begin to manipulate them.

Interior Versus Exterior

The most significant changes have come about in the relationship between interior spaces and exterior spaces such as streets, squares, the city, nature. Often, the interiors in which we live isolate rather than protect us from the outside world and are more like confined environments than enclosed environments. Living in a city means spending most of one's time in environments in which the fundamental characteristics of the natural environment have been artificially reproduced (according to Paul Machado, researcher at the National Health

(*Upper Right*): The Montclair Plaza Shopping Center, Los Angeles, California. (Photo: Norman Galper.)

An experiment to show the beneficial effects of wind. Sketch from Athanius Kircher, *Mundus subterraneus*, Amsterdam, Waesberge, 1665. (Courtesy of Biblioteca Trivulziana, Milan.)

"Il rebecchino in piazza Duomo," Amanzia Guerrilot, 1850, oil on canvas, Museo di Milano. (Photo: Archivio Fotografico di Milano.)

Council of Brasilia, we spend 80 percent of our life in enclosed environments).[3] Often, these environments seem to have been planned in deliberate contrast to the natural environment—in both the literal and metaphorical sense—rather than as its complement. This tendency, which is developing alongside the unfortunately progressive pollution of the earth's ecosystem, may in fact be directly linked to the latter phenomenon and interpreted as a gesture of self-defense on the part of human beings against a natural environment that is becoming increasingly dangerous. The importance of developing effective planning methodologies therefore cannot be overestimated. For it is one thing to plan spaces in natural environments and it is quite another to plan them in highly artificial environments (within large cities). It is one thing to plan spaces with windows and quite another to plan them without.

Environments Without Wind

The metropolis might be defined as the product of a new conception of city, and the shopping mall as the result of the

9

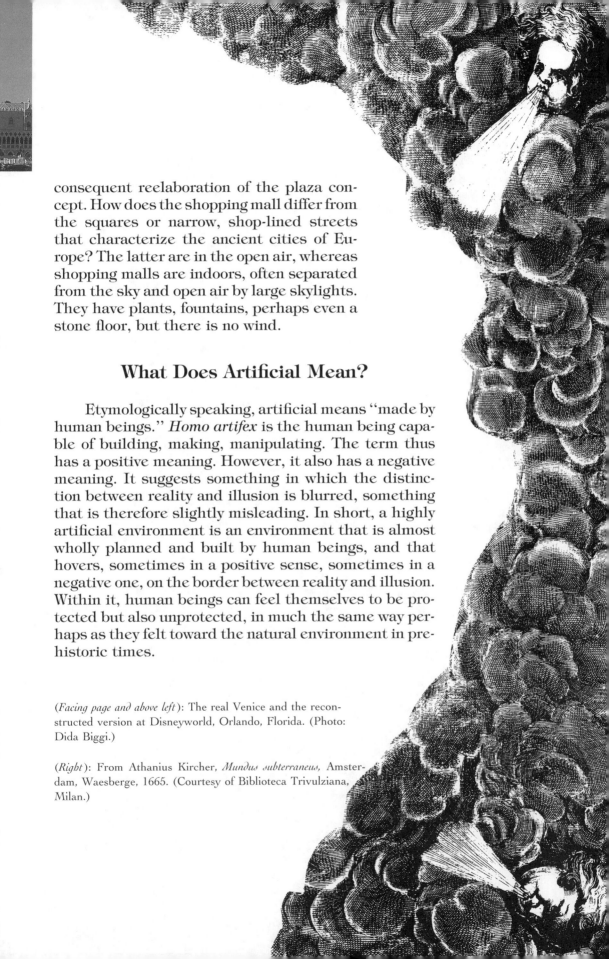

consequent reelaboration of the plaza concept. How does the shopping mall differ from the squares or narrow, shop-lined streets that characterize the ancient cities of Europe? The latter are in the open air, whereas shopping malls are indoors, often separated from the sky and open air by large skylights. They have plants, fountains, perhaps even a stone floor, but there is no wind.

What Does Artificial Mean?

Etymologically speaking, artificial means "made by human beings." *Homo artifex* is the human being capable of building, making, manipulating. The term thus has a positive meaning. However, it also has a negative meaning. It suggests something in which the distinction between reality and illusion is blurred, something that is therefore slightly misleading. In short, a highly artificial environment is an environment that is almost wholly planned and built by human beings, and that hovers, sometimes in a positive sense, sometimes in a negative one, on the border between reality and illusion. Within it, human beings can feel themselves to be protected but also unprotected, in much the same way perhaps as they felt toward the natural environment in prehistoric times.

(*Facing page and above left*): The real Venice and the reconstructed version at Disneyworld, Orlando, Florida. (Photo: Dida Biggi.)

(*Right*): From Athanius Kircher, *Mundus subterraneus*, Amsterdam, Waesberge, 1665. (Courtesy of Biblioteca Trivulziana, Milan.)

(*Facing page and above*): The rustic style lintel of a window in Palazzo Te illustrates the pronounced sensory nature of the materials used in sixteenth century Italian architecture. Loggia delle Muse, detail, Palazzo Te, Mantova, Italy, 1535. Architect: Giulio Romano. (Photo: Dida Biggi.)

(*Facing page, bottom*): Loggia delle Muse, Palazzo Te, Mantova, Italy, 1535. Architect: Giulio Romano. (Photo: Dida Biggi.)

Human-Artificial Beings

Homo artifex does not just manipulate the environment: He also manipulates the human organism. His interventions both on the body's exterior (plastic and aesthetic surgery, false teeth, eyeglasses, hair transplants) and interior (organ transplant, surrogate mothering, biological engineering, artificial insemination, using fetus cells) have become quite common practice, for both medical and aesthetic reasons (and, like everything else, for maniacal reasons as well). Even the psyche can be manipulated: Psychoanalysis helps neurotics by making them experience artificially created emotions and feelings. We are without doubt more artificial than our forebears, in the

sense that we are able to manipulate ourselves to a much greater extent.

Nowadays a woman can give birth to a child at an age that a few years ago would have been considered outrageous. Finally, it may be said with some satisfaction, that we have been able to lengthen our life span. The human beings of the year 2000 thus will be more artificial (and long-lived) than those who inhabited the earth in 1500 or 300 AD.

Detailed consideration of various aspects of our way of life broadens the discussion still further. Rarely is our life regulated by natural temporal rhythms. And here I am not speaking about rising when the cock crows or going to bed at sundown, or of eating strawberries in May and grapes in October. The experience of finding oneself in a context that is completely at odds with the one on which our organism is regulated has become quite common. It happens, for example, when we go on an intercontinental flight. In these situations,

(*Facing page, above and right*):
Views of Montecassiano, Italy.
(Photos: Piera Scuri.)

One of the many medieval villages that dot the landscape of central Italy. (Photo: Piera Scuri.)

which are now quite common but which nonetheless remain incredible, our organism finds itself working in a context that contradicts all the points of reference with which it is in synchronicity. Those who have experienced it will be familiar with the discomfort this causes. Of course, much of what has been stated up to now relates above all to certain cultures, certain societies, and certain parts of the earth. However, it is also true that the mass media and economic model created by multinationals have resulted in widespread diffusion of this trend.

Artificial Spaces for Mutating Organisms

If we compare some of Italy's medieval and Renaissance cities with today's cities, a strong contrast emerges. In comparison to the latter, ancient cities seem to have been planned almost as if they were the rooms of a house. The spatial configurations and architectural forms as a whole are considerate of the sensory aspect of the relationship between human be-

ings and space. There is, for example, an almost physical contact between skin and the walls lining the streets. Such feelings are particularly pronounced in the long and narrow *calli* of Venice or in certain little alleys of the medieval towns that dot the hills of Umbria, Tuscany, and the Marches. Steps,

(*Above and facing page*): Castle of Edinburgh, Scotland. (Photo: Douglas Skene.)

squares, and streets all have an almost intimate air. Their dimensions, proportions, and the materials used in their construction combine to create an atmosphere of familiarity, one that is simply on a human, or rather, organic scale.

Perhaps the most significant difference between these ancient cities and the modern city is the fact that the former are made up of spaces constructed to contain people and animals, not machines. And here the word machine should be understood in the widest sense, to include not just automobiles or other vehicles for transport, but also computers, air conditioners, televisions, etc. In the medieval and Renaissance eras, the city was within reach of not only the eyes, the organ that

permits space to be perceived from a distance, but also the skin, nose, and ears (bells, voices, bricks and stones, the smell of the air). The whole realm of the senses was stimulated.

Not that this is no longer true. Let us just say that it continues to be so, but in a different, and probably rather impoverished way. Some smells and noises are so predominant as to prevent us from perceiving an infinite variety of subtle smells and noises occurring in the environment, from the rustle of leaves in the wind to the smell of grass. In large

(*Above and facing page*): Artificial reconstruction of the earth's ecosystem, Kraft Pavilion, Epcot Center, Disneyworld, Orlando, Florida. (Photo: Dida Biggi.)

urban centers, the pealing of bells, if there is such a thing, is drowned out by much more powerful noises (the passage of an airplane, traffic, the hooting of horns, the sound of an elevator as it travels up and down, printers, or air conditioning units).

The characteristics (sensorially speaking) of the environments in which we live are profoundly different from those that characterized the interiors of even the last century, to say nothing of those of the eighteenth or sixteenth century. We could easily say that the intensity of sensorial stimuli has diminished significantly, both for better and for worse, in the sense that in winter we are less at the mercy of bitter winds, while in summer we suffer less from heat and humidity. But at the same time, we now hardly know the pleasure of the air touching our skin. Compared to the environments in which our grandparents lived, the environments in which we live are sensorially hypostimulatory. Or anyway different.

Take, for example, their chromatic quality. The research on this subject undertaken in Italy at the Montefibre Research Center in Milan in the 1970s is enlightening. Before the discovery of synthetic dyes in the nineteenth century, all colors

(*Left*): An experiment conducted by A. Kircher in the seventeenth century: artificial reconstruction of an optimal environment for plants in a glass bulb. Sketch from A. Kircher, *Ars magna lucis et umbrae*, Rome, apud Hermannum Scheus, 1646. (Courtesy of Biblioteca Trivulziana, Milan.)

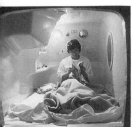

(*Left*): Microroom in a hotel, Tokyo, Japan. (Photo: Dida Biggi.)

were obtained from natural substances, such as plants, minerals, and animals. This meant that there was a greater homogeneity between the colors used for objects and spaces and those that occurred in nature. When instead it became possible to produce color by chemical means, an almost infinite range of chromatic possibilities was created.

Both the quality and use of color have also changed. According to the research conducted by Montefibre, the intermediate tonalities typical of presynthetic colors are now rarely used, having been replaced by strong, bold shades, saturated or nonsaturated colors (which increase product identity and market profile). The aims of color selection now differ widely from those of the preindustrial era.

Paint too is a recent discovery. Before, objects essentially retained the color of the material out of which they were made, whereas now it is fairly common practice to substitute the original color with another, produced artificially. This means that the chromatic quality of the environment has become an aspect in itself, as distinct from the characteristics of the materials of which it is constituted. It is created and produced by human beings (and is thus artificial).

Reconstruction of a marine environment, Epcot Center, Disneyworld, Orlando, Florida. (Photo: Dida Biggi.)

This fact has repercussions on the perceptual-mental level. Color (as Goethe states in his famous essay on the subject) mediates our relationship with the environment.[4] In other words, a "painted" environment tends toward a mental dimension and renders our relationship with it progressively less physical and spontaneous.[5] In light of these statements, let us try to imagine what type of message is transmitted to us by an environment consisting of raised walkways, double ceilings, movable walls, all made exclusively of synthetic materials.

Artificiality has always existed, practically since man first appeared on earth. It is the level of artificiality that changes, or rather increases. We might say that the level of artificiality is now very high and is apparent in very many aspects of the environments in which we live, from the physical to the symbolic. If the noises, smells, materials, forms, and colors of the environments in which we live have undergone profound changes, then so also have we.

The Solipsism Syndrome

Highly artificial environments influence the mental health of those who live in them and condition the type of in-

Reconstruction of a hypothetical agricultural settlement in the desert, Epcot Center, Disneyworld, Orlando, Florida. (Photo: Dida Biggi.)

teraction and social organization carried on inside them. This is the theory of researchers at the NASA's Ames Research Center who are working toward a definition of planning parameters for settlements in outer space. They emphasize the importance of what they call the "solipsism syndrome in an artificial environment": that is, the fact that such environments create an unreal mental state. They describe this as being a highly uncomfortable psychological state, causing people to feel "lonely and detached, apathetic and indifferent." Sufferers do not simply feel sad, but experience a very precise sensation caused by a loss of contact with reality and by taking refuge within oneself. The description of this psychological state continues:

> Some environments are conducive to the state of
> mind in which a person feels that everything is a dream
> and is not real. This state of mind occurs, for example,
> in the Arctic winter when it is night 24 hr a day. . . . A
> person feels very lonely and detached, and eventually be-
> comes apathetic and indifferent. In the small town of
> Lund, Sweden, the winter days have 6 hr of daylight
> and 18 hr of darkness. Most of the time people live under
> artificial light, so that life acquires a special quality. Out-
> doors, there is no landscape to see; only street corners
> lit by lamps. These street corners look like theater stages,
> detached from one another. There is no connectedness or
> depth in the universe and it acquires a very unreal quality
> as though the whole world is imagination. . . . This state
> of mind can be easily produced in an environment where ev-
> erything is artificial, where everything is like a theater
> stage, where every wish can be fulfilled by a push-button,
> and where there is nothing beyond the theater stage and
> beyond an individual's control.[6]

This research carried out by NASA makes an important point: An artificial environment communicates a precise set of information and stimuli, or rather, stimuli-information. The human organism intercepts these and reacts accordingly. The artificial environment thus influences our way of life, our life itself, just as much as the natural environment. This research concerns in a direct way work environments destined for outer space, but indirectly, it concerns both existing city scenarios as well as those that are coming into being.

Without Culture

Many of the city environments in which we work, shop, or eat our meals are decontextualized. That is to say, they might be anywhere: Paris, Los Angeles, or Berlin. Whether offices, shopping centers, or restaurants, the cultural aspect is often undervalued. And the problem assumes even more importance in those environments that, thanks to the presence of technology, may lead one mistakenly to think of their adoption as standardized. Failing to consider the cultural needs of human beings means strengthening the presence of artificiality, in a different, but very negative, way. It means forcing people to behave in a way that is artificial.

Of course, artificial behavior is not as serious as having smallpox or tuberculosis, or any one of those terrible maladies of the preindustrial era. However, it does force people to live badly, which, if possible, is better to avoid. On this count, it is worthwhile noting that in a field in which communication and therefore the cultural dimension are very important, the latter point is often ignored. Such is the case of office spaces. The office systems of the Herman Miller Company, for example, make not the slightest concession to the national boundaries of various countries: Their points of reference instead consist of a number of cities strategically situated in different parts of the world.

Wet 'n' Wild, Amusement Park, Orlando, Florida. (Photo: Dida Biggi.)

Amusement Parks and Boudoirs

Perfect examples of "artificial environments" are provided by the numerous pavillions at the Epcot Center, Disneyworld, Orlando, Florida. These are technological prodigies on a small scale, created in order to artificially produce certain predetermined sensations and emotional states (all big amusement parks are, as a rule, ingenious and extremely sophisticated machines built to induce pleasant sensations by means of special "euphoria-producing" techniques: simulation, miniaturization, the use of special effects, the blurring of reality with fantasy, the negation of time and death, etc.). Among the various techniques employed with the aim of producing euphoria, pleasure, excitement, surprise, etc., simulation perhaps takes pride of place. The reconstructions of streets, squares, and buildings of countries like China, Italy, Morocco, France, and Canada, for example, are simulations. They constitute so many small-scale environments, accurately reconstructed, albeit not from a philological point of view. (the bell tower of St. Mark's in Venice, e.g., is in a different place from the original). Rather than being exact copies, what they tend to do is to create the same atmosphere. And in certain cases, they succeed: The Mexican pavilion allows one to forget for a moment that one is actually in Florida. For a few magic seconds, one feels transported into another dimension. It is possible to eat local dishes and buy the products of "local" craftsmen. The space, dimensions, objects, and forms (and in the restaurants, the smells) allow one to lose contact with and escape from reality. Miniaturization is a special type of simulation, in that it reproduces reality, but on a reduced scale. Reducing reality to a small and charming object is a way of dedramatizing it, and as a result, euphoria is produced. It acts as a sort of exorcism of feelings such as fear that often plague our life. Disneyworld is a window onto some of the desires and fears of American society (and of those societies influenced by it).

A rather striking contrast was provided by the boudoir in eighteenth century France. This too was conceived as a place of pleasure but its characteristics differed somewhat from those of Disneyworld. However, these two environments have one feature in common: the use of simulation. A detailed description of the boudoir is provided by Camus de Mezières:

> The boudoir is regarded as the abode of sensual delight, where plans may be mediated and natural inclinations followed. It is essential for everything to be treated in a style in which luxury, softness and good taste predominate. . . . One should at all costs avoid the hard, crude shadows thrown by lighting that is too vivid. The light should be mysterious: this will be obtained by placing mirrors over part of the casements. Openings and repetitions may be produced in abundance by means of mirrors. But see to it that they do not form the bulk of the furnishings. Too many of them will make the room seem bleak and monotonous. . . . If the casements are to the east, the light will be softer; as far as possible they should look out on favourable views; however, in the absence of Nature herself, have recourse to Art. This is where taste and genius should be displayed to the full: every resource must be brought into play, using the magic of painting and perspective to create illusions. . . . The boudoir would be all the more delightful if the recess where the bed is placed were provided with mirrors; the joints could be concealed by carved tree-trunks, gathered skillfully in leafy masses and painted after Nature. The repetition would form a quinconce, multiplied in the mirrors. The visual effect would be enhanced by an arrangement of candles and gauze hangings, some stretched tightly, others floating loose, to produce a graduated light. The boudoir would seem like a grove of trees, and painted statues distributed appropriately would add to the charm and the illusion.[7]

This strange association between the amusement park of
the year 2000 and the eighteenth century place of pleasure
shows the extent to which the use of the simulated environ-

Reconstruction of Paris, Epcot Center, Disneyworld, Orlando, Florida. (Photo:
Dida Biggi.)

ment has changed and spread in the course of two centuries. If in the eighteenth century, artifice was destined primarily for adults, producing very special, almost prohibited places, on the threshold of the year 2000, it has invaded the world of the child.

CHAPTER 2

ISOLATED AND CONFINED ENVIRONMENTS

Launch pad at Kennedy Space Center, Orlando, Florida. (Photo: Dida Biggi.)

Surviving

Except perhaps for some ocean abysses, there are no longer any unexplored areas left on our planet. And there are few that have not yet been manipulated by human beings. Naturally, the level of artifice (or manipulation) is very high in certain places, for example, in very large cities, where the environment is almost wholly man-made. We are even able artificially to reproduce light and air! But this also signifies that we are designing environmental elements that have an effect on profound and delicate aspects of the organism. As if in the wake of a powerful regressive phenomenon (and after some members of the human species were capable of building such architectural masterpieces as Venice), we are now designing vital environmental elements that it was once the job of nature to provide. In other words, we have gone back to dealing with problems regarding survival. This, from a technological point of view, undoubtedly constitutes a victory, but from an architectural point of view undoubtedly represents significant regression. If in the past it was possible to compose poems with space, the problem now seems to have become that of defining an alphabet or a grammar. What should be the source of the new letters and the new grammatical rules? The solutions must, of necessity, come from the study of the human organism, and from the way in which this organism lives and perceives.

Space agencies throughout the world are now engaged in the careful study of the relationship between the human organism and space. They have been doing so since the very first missions to outer space. The aim, naturally, is to succeed in protecting not only the life, but also the work capacity of human beings in extremely difficult environmental conditions. To this end, numerous studies have been carried out in special earth environments called analogues, which reproduce environmental conditions similar to those in spacecraft and space stations. From submarines, to polar laboratories, to underground spaces, pressure chambers, and offshore platforms, analogues are basically environments that are isolated, confined, and have a high technological profile. Such studies also

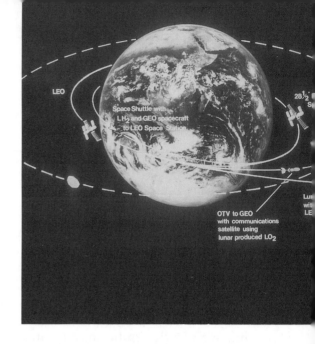

Labels in image: LEO, Space Shuttle with LH$_2$ and GEO spacecraft to LEO Space Station, 28½° S, OTV to GEO with communications satellite using lunar produced LO$_2$, Lu wit LE

(*Above and facing page*): Possible flight trajectories for the transport of oxygen from the earth to the moon. The drawing shows one of the hypotheses developed for the Johnson Space Center by Eagle Engineering. Drawing by Pat Rawlings. (Courtesy of NASA.)

offer valuable material—unobtainable by other means—for planning environments on the earth. In fact, extreme situations can often render visible aspects that in normal situations are invisible (this is why so much brain research is conducted on brain disorders). The current tendency toward an ever more artificial dimension makes us suppose that the studies carried out in the analogues may, by making them extreme, clarify certain aspects of contemporary environments and prefigure those of the future.

Space Flights

Voyages into outer space are a rich source of information. Precisely because of its abnormal nature, the environment of outer space illustrates the importance for our organism of certain characteristics of the planet upon which we live, such as the presence of gravity and of a particular space-time dimension. An excellent description of this is given in *Perception of Space and Time in Outer Space* by A. Aleksei Leonov and

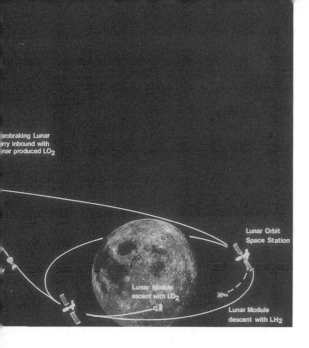

erobraking Lunar
rry inbound with
nar produced LO$_2$

Lunar Orbit
Space Station

Lunar Module
ascent with LO$_2$

Lunar Module
descent with LH$_2$

Valentin Lebedev, translated by NASA shortly after its publication in 1968:

> . . . During an interplanetary flight, an astronaut's perception of speed disappears completely. A uniform picture lies be-

Touchdown of the shuttle at the space station. Drawing of Rockwell International concept. (Courtesy of NASA.)

fore him. In one porthole, he sees bright, non-flickering stars against the background of a sky which is as black as ink; in the other porthole, he sees the blindingly bright disc of the never-setting sun. Thus, astronauts sense an excess of time while the craft moves away from celestial bodies. On the other hand, when approaching some celestial body or the Earth, there is a time deficit.[8]

In outer space, the earth's spatial reference system, in which the whole of the human organism—skeleton, muscles, perceptual apparatus, nervous system, etc.—has been formed, disappears. The absence of gravity means that there is no longer an above and a below, a right or a left. The temporal sequence of the earth is also missing (morning, midday, afternoon, evening, autumn, spring, winter, sun, rain, snow, wind, etc.). Unless the spaceship is nearing or moving away from a planet, the images outside the cockpit during space flights are immobile. The disorientation produced in the human body by the lack of normal, earthly spatial-temporal references thus constitutes a serious problem.

The problems faced by astronauts from takeoff to touchdown are numerous and complex. This is why so much importance is given to training on the ground and to the psychological and physiological state of the individuals making up the crew. Astronauts are first and foremost pilots whose task is to navigate what are often very complex flight paths, and who may (as was the case for both the Soviets and Americans) be forced to land their craft manually if the electronic equipment fails. In addition, unexpected problems may arise during an interplanetary flight that, by their very nature, cannot be dealt with by the instruments on board. Problems of this type have to be resolved by human beings, since machines are able only to carry out those tasks for which they were programmed. It is thus vitally important that astronauts maintain good equilibrium and above all a good sense of direction during flights in outer space.

The Soviet space station MIR in orbit in 1986. The ex-Soviets introduced several modifications to working environments for outer space. Inside MIR, instruments were concealed behind panels and different colors (yellow and green) used to differentiate the eating area from the working area. (Photo: Dida Biggi.)

Space Stations (MIR and Freedom): Living Quarters

The design of the living module in space stations is extremely important. It is not enough just to build airtight containers and supply them with air, water, light, heating, and food. Rather, an environment must be created that is capable of protecting the astronauts' health and psychological well-being. One way of doing this is by creating a spatial-temporal reference system which substitutes, at least in part, that of the earth. The numerous space flights undertaken by the former Soviet Union have provided Soviet researchers with a vast body of information regarding the reactions of the human body to unfamiliar environmental conditions. The first data were gathered during Yuri Gagarin's flight in 1961. Glavcosmos has had a permanently manned base in space since 1986. MIR belongs to the third generation of space stations built by the former Soviet Union and is basically a reelaboration of Salyut, the first version of which was launched in 1971. (A new space station, MIR 2, is currently being planned.) The modifications made to the interior of MIR's living module are a result of the recognition of the importance of this environment for the astronaut.

The Salyut 7 mission of 1984 (during which two astronauts lived in space for eight months) demonstrated that the major source of stress for the crew was of a psychological nature, and the living quarters were found to be in part responsible for causing it. A well-planned arrangement of the interior can attenuate the difficult environmental conditions that characterize it: lack of privacy, continual noise, high levels of risk, enclosed space of tiny dimensions, the presence of unknown sensorial stimuli, the absence of spatial-temporal reference points. MIR has none of the cumbersome scientific equipment that took up so much room in the space stations that preceded it. The tangled mass of wires and ducts that "decorated" the interior of the Salyut version has been hidden behind yellow and green panels. The interior has been divided up into dif-

(*Below*): Artist's impression of facilities for life science experiments. (Courtesy of NASA.)

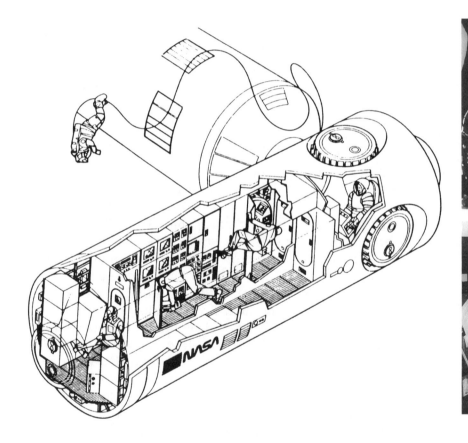

(*Upper right and facing page*): Interior of an American spaceship during a mission. This, according to the Habitability Research Group of NASA's Ames Research Center, is a bad example of living quarters in space because of the overcrowding of technological apparatus that has also been left entirely visible. (Courtesy of NASA.)

(*Lower right and facing page*): Surveying physiological data during a European spacelab laboratory mission. (Courtesy of Alenia Spazio.)

ferent areas, including one for eating, furnished with a table
and food warmers. Each crew member has a small personal
space of his or her own, with a window, bed, table, and chair.
In order to lessen the sense of confinement, false windows have
been painted on the inside walls. A variable lighting system has
been developed that introduces a temporal rhythm to the environment. The sense of an "above" and a "below" has been

given by painting one side of the cabin in a dark
shade (the floor) and the opposite side in a lighter
shade (the ceiling). In order to combat acoustic
monotony, the astronauts can listen to a series of
recordings that reproduce some of the noises
heard on earth, such as the patter of rain, a bird-
song, etc.

Space agencies are currently working on
plans for the manned mission to Mars that will
involve a prolonged stay in space (the return jour-
ney alone will probably take as long as three
years). Personnel training programs have already
begun, and at the same time, studies are being
carried out on the characteristics that the spaceship environment must have in order for the
mission to succeed. The Soviet experience has
demonstrated the importance of environmental
simulation in permitting astronauts to remain in
space for several months and maintain their capacity to work as well as their lucidity. On returning to earth, three weeks seems to be sufficient
time for their reintegration to normal life.

The design of the living quarters of the space
station Freedom has been the subject of much
research by NASA. One such study was that conducted at the Ames Research Center during the
1980s by the Habitability Research Group. From this, a series
of planning parameters was defined, or rather, certain modifications were suggested in order to reduce the problems—
above all, those of a psychological nature—experienced by
astronauts. Some examples of these were the use of fab-
rics whose color and pattern change according to the light
as a means of increasing sensory stimuli; using colors in

such a way as to allow the perception of an above and a below, thus reducing the problems created by disorientation; the introduction of mirrors and fake windows in order to allow the perception of depth and attenuate the sense of confinement; fixing a plaque with the astronaut's name on the door of his or her cabin, together with some magnetic boards on which to write or stick personal objects, in order to strengthen the sense of individual territory. These are minor contrivances that seem nevertheless to assume great importance from a psychological point of view.

Many experiments have been conducted by the Habitability Research Group with the aim of evaluating how many and which photographs should be used to decorate the walls of the living module. According to NASA researchers, photographs of animals, flowers, and people are important since they help maintain contact with the earth's environment, whereas photographs of landscapes and buildings allow even the inhabitant of a tiny cabin to perceive depth.

Note how the solutions advanced by NASA reveal the profession of its researchers, for the most part psychologists. There is no room for architects in outer space. Or at least not yet. However, both architects and the architectural departments of universities are currently engaged in defining planning parameters for possible future colonies in outer space, studying the design of both living quarters for spaceships and space stations, as well as settlements on the moon or Mars.[9] The knowledge on which their studies are based is still at a theoretical or experimental level, but is potentially very useful, and not just for its applications in outer space.

Analogues

One of the areas much studied by space agencies is that of simulation in the pursuit of which, so-called analogues are used. These are places that allow the study of problems encountered by the human organism in confined, high-tech environments. For example, some fascinating studies into visual perception have been conducted in submarines, where it has been demonstrated that long stays in confined environments have a detrimental effect on visual ability because of the lack of "deep vanishing points." As a consequence, researchers advise that when planning these sorts of spaces/machines, allowance should be made for the creation of "distant visual centers of interest," perhaps even adopting illusionistic techniques. The use of mirrors and tromp l'oeil, both of which encourage the perception of depth, is advised in all confined spaces. Research conducted in underground environments and polar regions has shown how sunlight influences our organism. Other important sources of information about the problems caused by isolation and interaction with advanced technology include pressure chambers, offshore platforms,

Artist's impression of lunar mining operations for producing liquid oxygen. Artist: Pat Rawlings. (Photo: NASA.)

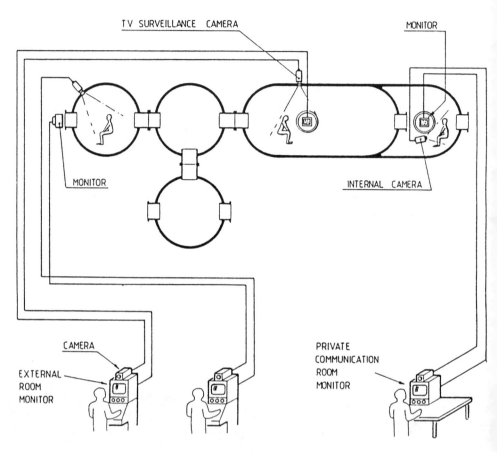

TV SURVEILLANCE CAMERA

MONITOR

MONITOR

INTERNAL CAMERA

CAMERA

EXTERNAL
ROOM
MONITOR

PRIVATE
COMMUNICATION
ROOM
MONITOR

Experiment in a pressure chamber. A 1:1 simulation of a space mission. Technical adaptations: video communication. COMEX HYDRA IX experiment, 1989. (Courtesy of ESA.)

and spacecraft. Pressure chambers and underwater laboratories (such as Aquarius) are very similar to space habitats, in that they too are, in a certain sense, nonterrestial. In both cases, the fundamental problem is that of the successful reproduction of air.[10]

Studies of confined environments are important because they illustrate the role played by the natural environment in maintaining the equilibrium of our organism. The human body is regulated by stimuli produced by the natural environment. These stimuli regard above all time—time in the sense of a vital rhythm. Light, air,

COMFORT

FALSE PERSPECTIVE
PORTHOLE

LIBRARY FOR
VCR
HI FI SOUND SYSTEM
BOOKS

the changing plant world: Every day, our organism is regulated by this remarkable clock, capable of communicating with us and stimulating our perceptive-sensory apparatus even through the walls of houses, windows, doors, verandas, balconies, terraces, skylights, etc. The stimuli produced by a confined environment prompt a seriously disturbed reaction from the human organism. The perceptual apparatus itself is modified by such an environment. When the stimuli normally produced by natural light (and air) are missing, the organism undergoes a process of desynchronization and repercussions are felt at various levels, from the cognitive to the cellular. For this reason, it is vital, in the planning of highly artificial environments to bear in mind the psycho-physiological mechanisms of perception.

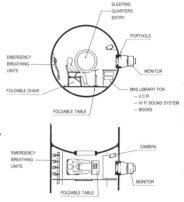

(*Below left and facing page*): Experiment in a pressure chamber. A 1:1 simulation of a space mission. Arrangement of living quarters. COMEX HYDRA IX experiment, 1989. (Courtesy of ESA.)

(*Below right*): Experiment in a pressure chamber. Simulation. COMEX HYDRA IX experiment, 1989. (Courtesy of ESA.)

(*Above right*): Experiment in a pressure chamber. A 1:1 simulation of a space mission. Arrangement of private communications room. COMEX HYDRA IX experiment, 1989. (Courtesy of ESA.)

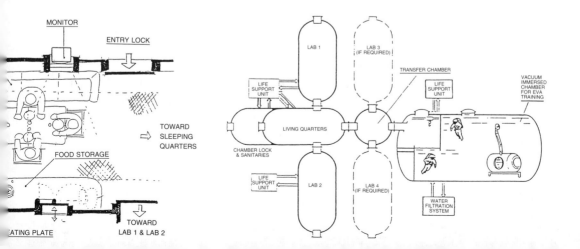

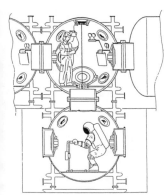

A New Biotope

The biotope in which we live is almost entirely of our own creation (and although certainly not to the

(*Left*): Experiment in a pressure chamber. A 1:1 simulation of a space mission. Working activities. COMEX HYDRA IX experiment, 1989. (Courtesy of ESA.)

(*Below*): Experiment in a pressure chamber. Simulation of underwater habitat with crew transfer submarine. COMEX HYDRA IX experiment, 1989. (Courtesy of ESA.)

extent seen in space stations or rockets, the tendency to exert total control over our environment is one that undoubtedly exists). The creation of this biotope was a task that called for a profound knowledge of the laws that regulate our organism.

(*Upper right*): Aquarius underwater laboratory, an analogue at Salt River Canyon, St. Croix, Caribbean Sea, about 4000 meters below sea level. (Photo: Douglas Smith.)

(*Lower right*): Aquanauts inside the Aquarius cockpit. (Photo: Douglas Smith.)

The planning of highly technological environments must take into account the needs of human beings. In fact, though, the environments and spaces in which we spend our lives are quite unsuited to the multiple needs of an organism that has evolved in close contact with nature. First and foremost is the problem of the artificial reproduction of air and light. The techniques developed to date may be adequate in situations where they are integrated on a temporary basis with natural air and light, but they cannot substitute for them for very long. The human organism is an open system, constantly influenced by the environment and constantly adapting to it. Our senses are the product of a natural selection that has taken place within the earth's ecosystem over a period of thousands of years. The fact that we now suddenly find ourselves living in highly artificial environments cannot but have important consequences. Actually, the situation involves some risks that it would be to our advantage to recognize. These risks are linked, for example, to the perception of time (which tends to be deformed by exposure to artificial light and air) and sensory stimuli (which are greatly reduced in an artificial environment).

Reflections on the Planning of Artificial Environments

Underground spaces are used for a wide variety of work activities (for housing offices, hospitals, health clubs, bookshops, supermarkets, schools, etc.). However, this fact does not seem to attract much notice. And indeed, the actual form

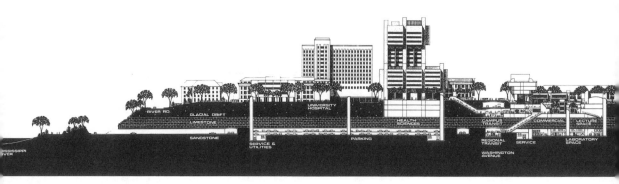

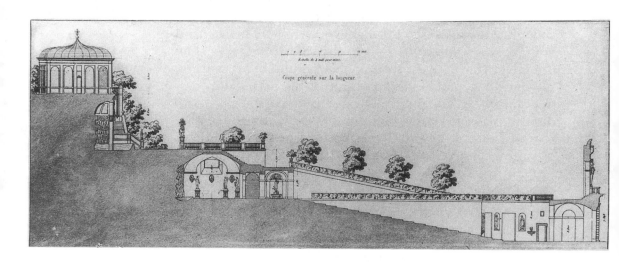

Coupe générale sur la longueur.

RIVER RD. · LABORATORY & LECTURE SPACE · CAMPUS TRANSIT · THE MALL · CHURCH STREET · GLACIAL DRIFT · LIMESTONE · SANDSTONE · UNION ST. · LECTURE SPACE · LECTURE SPACE · STORAGE & SERVICE

SERVICE & UTILITIES · PARKING · LABORATORY SPACE

MISSISSIPPI RIVER

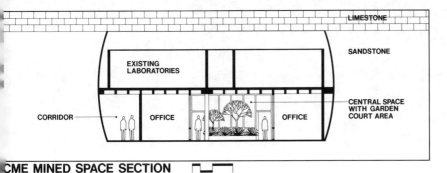

LIMESTONE

SANDSTONE

EXISTING LABORATORIES

CENTRAL SPACE WITH GARDEN COURT AREA

CORRIDOR · OFFICE · OFFICE

CME MINED SPACE SECTION
FIGURE 3

0 2 5 10

CME MINED SPACE PLAN
FIGURE 2

COMPLETION OF UNFINISHED MINED SPACE IN CME BUILDING DESIGN: JOHN CARMODY

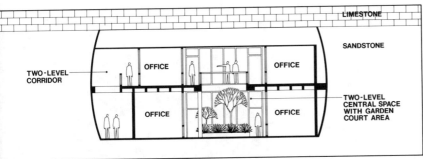

LIMESTONE

SANDSTONE

TWO-LEVEL CORRIDOR

OFFICE · OFFICE

OFFICE · OFFICE

TWO-LEVEL CENTRAL SPACE WITH GARDEN COURT AREA

TWO-LEVEL MINED SPACE CONCEPT
FIGURE 4

0 2 5 10

(*Above*): Plan of unfinished mined space in CME Building, Minneapolis, Minnesota, 1977. BRW Architects. (Courtesy of John Carmody.)

(*Left*): Section of unfinished mined space in CME Building, Minneapolis, Minnesota, 1977. BRW Architects. (Courtesy of John Carmody.)

(*Above top and facing page, top*): Sections of Civil and Mineral Engineering Building at the University of Minnesota, Minneapolis, 1977. BRW Architects. (Courtesy of John Carmody.)

(*Facing page, middle*): Cross section of interior of Vignola's Orti Farnesiani. From P. Letarouilly, *Edifices de Rome moderne*, Liège, D'Avanzo, 1853. (Courtesy of Biblioteca d'Arte Castello Sforzesco, Milan.)

(*Facing page, bottom*): View of Interior of Vignola's Orti Farnesiani. From P. Letarouilly, *Edifices de Rome moderne*, Liège, D'Avanzo, 1853. (Courtesy of Biblioteca d'Arte Castello Sforzesco, Milan.)

(*Above and facing page top*): International Watch Museum, La Chaux de Fonds, Switzerland. Architects: Pierre Zoelly and George J. Haefeli. Photo: Georg Staerk. (Courtesy of Pierre Zoelly.)

(*Right and facing page bottom*): Iconographical representation of an early Christian church built on the model of the catacombs. Visible here are the tiny apertures through which light was let into such underground churches. From A. Bosio, *Roma sotterranea*, Rome, Facciotti, 1632. (Courtesy of Biblioteca d'Arte, Milan.)

these environments take is rarely indicative of their peculiar nature, their subterranean condition. They have no windows and access is gained by several flights of stairs or an elevator, but these are the only concessions to the unique nature of this particular type of environment. As for furnishings, materials employed, lighting, and spatial configuration, no substantial difference exists with those found above ground, on the first or third floor (with the exception of some underground buildings in Finland, in which the natural rock has been left visible to form magnificent walls). No acknowledgment is made of the subterranean condition of such environments. This failure to acknowledge life in underground spaces leads us to make some considerations of a cultural nature. In fact, underground space is a space associated with death. It therefore cannot avoid evoking an idea, a reality that our society tends to reject. (There is also, of course, an economic factor: To pretend that these spaces do not exist allows one to avoid the question of how best to construct them.) However, to give such little consideration to underground spaces means doing similarly on the ground level. It means to freeze reality in an illusory, static, nonvital dimension. Consequently, the effects of such unnatural conditions are not even analyzed, nor is the potential of underground buildings exploited.

In 1977, the Underground Space Center was set up at the University of Minneapolis, its aim being to conduct research and further studies on the subject of building underground, as well as to gather and provide information about it. Its offices are situated 35 meters underground, in a building designed specifically to demonstrate the potential savings of energy and space by building underground. As researchers at the Underground Space Center have shown, the advantages of building underground are numerous (lower energy consumption, protection from natural or human disasters, the possibility of utilizing spaces that would otherwise be unsuitable for building, high levels of acoustic insulation, extremely strong struc-

Frontispiece of a seventeenth century text on the underground architecture of early Christian Rome. From A. Bosio, *Roma sotterranea*, Rome, Facciotti, 1632. (Courtesy of Biblioteca d'Arte, Milan.)

ROMA SOTTERRANEA

In Roma appreffo Gugliclmo Facciotti MDCXXXII con licenza de Superiori.
e priuilegio

tures, etc.). The same researchers also acknowledge, however, that there are distinct disadvantages, some of which concern the psychological and physiological effects on the human body caused by living and working underground.[11]

To construct work spaces underground in the same way as work spaces on the second floor of a building, without emphasizing the differences or signalling the points where the two overlap, means to ignore the communicative function of space. And while the use of certain illusionistic devices in underground environments, and confined environments in general, is necessary (e.g., by the strategic positioning of mirrors in order to create the illusion of a bigger space), it is, however, equally important from a cognitive point of view to "know where one is."

In order for an organism to function and be productive, it needs to be in a suitable environment. It is quite possible to provide such an environment underground, but only when the peculiarities of such an environment—that is, the fact that it is special—are given due consideration. This has to be done at the planning and design stage.[12] Underground work spaces must be laid out in a certain way and the people who work in them must adhere to certain patterns of behavior (it is important, e.g., that they spend their rest periods above ground). The way in which the space is organized, the type of furnishings, and most important the lighting should all be directed at helping people maintain contact with reality, with the outside. Confined environments in general and underground work environments in particular are becoming increasingly common, thanks to the introduction of new tech nologies. But these same new tech-

(*Above left, top*): Subway station exit in Frankfurt, Germany. (Photo: Douglas Skene.)

(*Above left, bottom*): New York subway interior. (Photo: Dida Biggi.)

Frontispiece to a seventeenth century text on the forces governing the earth. From A. Kircher, *Mundus subterraneus*, Amsterdam, Waesberge, 1665. (Courtesy of Biblioteca Trivulziana, Milan.)

nologies may also in the future reveal themselves to be very valuable in lessening the stress created by highly artificial environmental conditions.

Offshore Platforms

In every part of the world, offshore platforms emerge from the seas like gigantic metal icebergs, anchored to the sea bed by complex scaffolding or floating on the surface. They can appear, when looked at from afar or in a photograph, quite beautiful in their setting of a majestic tropical sunset or an ice-bound sea. However, as spaces for containing human organisms, they are, like all spaces with high levels of technology, extremely stressful. In the same way, large cities may also create beautiful images, with their proud skyscrapers in profile against the sky and the color effects produced by lights and headlights of moving cars, yet, at the same time, they may actually be hellish spaces. Offshore platforms are isolated working environments (linked to the mainland by a ferry or helicopter, depending on their distance from the coast) and in part confined. This is especially true of platforms in the North Sea, where, because of the harsh environmental conditions, the living quarters are often devoid of windows. As working environments, they are cramped and psychologically taxing.[13] Problems vary depending on the geographical situation of the platform (whether in arctic or equatorial seas); its size (some are quite small, in which case staff only stay on them for the time it takes to install the equipment, whereas others may accommodate hundreds of workers); its function (platforms are actually small industrial complexes for the extraction of gas or oil). Platforms vary in type as well as the sort of activity they carry out; the amount of accessible space they contain; the number of people that work on them, their nationality, and race. But basically, the biggest problem faced by operators is stress caused by confinement, isolation, and interaction with advanced technologies.

Offshore platforms are considered to be "analogues," and as such are the subject of study by space agencies. The Euro-

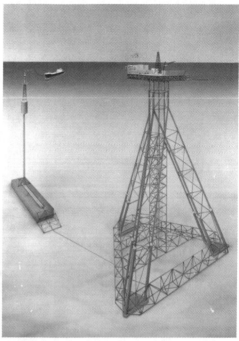

Offshore platform designed by Tecnomare. (Courtesy of Tecnomare.)

pean Space Agency, for example, has commissioned the setting up of a database to record the incidence of illnesses and accidents on North Sea platforms over a ten-year period. Four thousand cases have been analyzed in order to define the parameters for crew selection and training.[14] Such studies may also prove very useful in the planning of these structures. Offshore platforms constitute a sort of prototype for future marine-based working environments such as artificial islands, underwater laboratories and tunnels. It is possible to think of them as fragments of a new type of space that technology enables us to steal from science fiction and build. They may be useful for both elaborating more advanced planning techniques as well as testing them.

Confined environments all have one characteristic in common: the presence of advanced technologies. That is to say, without the required technological means we could not absent ourselves for a long time from the natural dimension without risking our very lives. In this sense, technology is truly a means

A hypothetical space colony. (Courtesy of NASA.)

(*Facing page*): Design for a hypothetical space colony: Plan for an apartment; housing; view of the interior. (Courtesy of NASA.)

by which human capacity and potential may be increased, but
only if it is used more often to promote our health and well-
being.

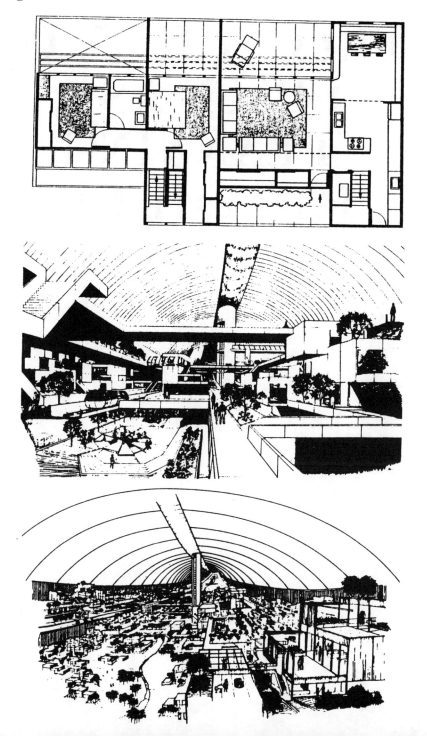

CHAPTER 3

THE PERCEPTION OF SPACE AS A PLANNING PARAMETER

Modern man is now in a position in which he is able
to give shape to almost everything in the world he inhabits;
our cities are creating new types of people in their slums,
mental hospitals, prisons and suburbs. But considering
"how little we know of man" it is frightening to think that
we are determining "the kind of organism" that will
inhabit the future. This is the basis for my present inquiry:
I want to look especially at the distances established
between animals, to examine their need, that is, to
demarcate their own territory, to exercise dominion over
an area of land, thus conditioning their behaviour, their
level of aggressivity, and the degree to which they can
tolerate overcrowded environments; I want then to look
at the human receptors, from immediate ones such as the
sense of smell, the skin and the muscles to the more
evolved ones of hearing and sight. This will be followed
by analyses of "thermic space," "tactile space," and
"visual space".

Sight, hearing, touch, smell, thermic receptors, kinematic
aesthetics: each of the senses makes its own contribution
to the perception of space. . . . Architects have a well
developed sense of natural architecture, of the harmony between living space and environment; but today what is
needed is a human architecture designed, like shoes and
clothes, to fit not only the human body, but its "space bub-
bles" as well.

Only by adopting a scientific approach in the creation of
spaces can architects find a way out of the present impasse,
opening up new possibilities that are a departure from Beaux
Arts precepts.[15]

THE PHYSIOLOGICAL LEVEL

The perception of space is a very complex phenomenon in that it regards not only the perception of the surroundings

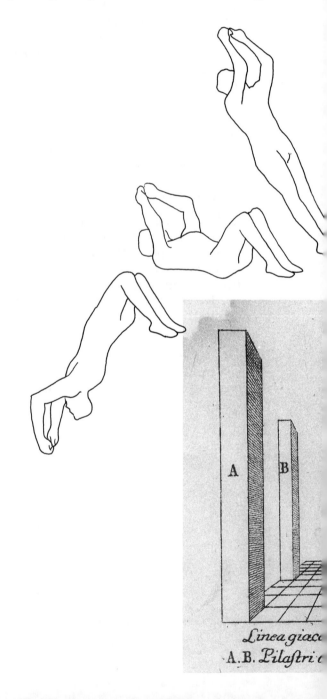

Linea giace
A.B. Pilaſtri

(*Below top, and facing page, top*): Weightlessness. Drawing by Temma Katsuya.

(*Below bottom, and facing page, bottom*): Perspectival drawing by Leonardo da Vinci. From *Trattato della pittura di Leonardo da Vinci nuovamente dato in luce con la vita dell'autore stesso scritta da Raffael du Fresne*, Bologna, Istituto delle Scienze, 1786. (Courtesy of Biblioteca Comunale, Milan.)

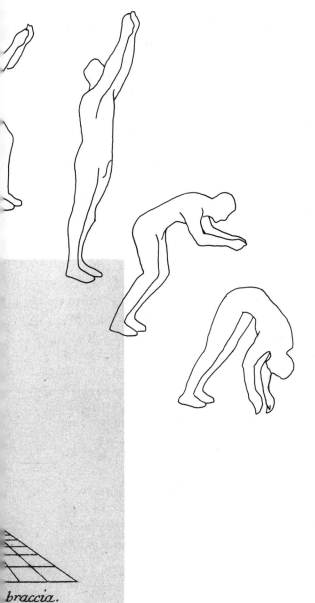

braccia.

ieci braccia.

(forms, images, objects), but has primarily to do with the way we balance our body and move around (walking, sitting, turning, bending).

It is difficult to rationalize our relationship with space because it is difficult clearly to distinguish the borders between our body and our surroundings: between the "inside" and the "outside." And this holds true at many levels. For example, only through experience do we learn to distance images from our eyes and attribute depth to them. This is proved by the accounts of blind people who regain their sight in adulthood. Thanks to their sense of touch, the blind are able to form a very clear idea of spatial dimensions. But upon regaining their sight, they have the sensation that the space surrounding them is full of objects, and that what they see touches their eyes. As they move about, they are afraid of colliding with these objects. In other words, they must learn to project the optical image onto the surrounding world. And in fact, what is meant by the perception of space is an intricate mixture of stimuli and feelings, concepts and sentiments that are difficult to single out and separate, even only in terms of whether they originate from the interior or exterior.[16]

Within the perceptual system, two levels may be roughly distinguished: the physiological level and the psychological level. The former concerns the way in which our body adapts to (and counters) the force of gravity and intercepts the stimuli of electromagnetic and mechanical energy. In a certain sense, it is the zero level of our relationship with space. The latter involves the complex elaboration made by our psyche of the data it receives from the perceptual system. This level may in its turn be subdivided into a series of subcategories (emotional, affective, cultural, cognitive, symbolic, etc.).

To make such a distinction between physiological and psychological aspects is imprecise and arbitrary, in that it separates phenomena that in reality are closely connected. This is seen in the fact that an architectural form (whether the ogives of a gothic cathedral or the cupolas of Renaissance churches) can only carry out its symbolic function after it has

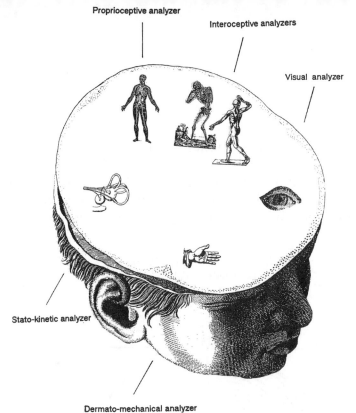

Proprioceptive analyzer

Interoceptive analyzers

Visual analyzer

Stato-kinetic analyzer

Dermato-mechanical analyzer

The sensory analyzers. (Photomontage: Donatella Ravizza.)

been intercepted by the visual apparatus. It does, however, allow us (and this is the point) to begin unravelling the intricate pattern of stimuli, sensations, emotions, feelings, and concepts that we call the perception of space.

The Sensory Analyzers

According to some enlightening studies conducted in the 1960s by Dr. Valentin Lebedev and the astronaut Aleksei Leonov, the human being perceives space through the interaction of a series of sensory analyzers that intercept messages coming from both inside and outside our body.[17] The exteroceptive analyzers pick up electromagnetic energy (light and sound) and mechanical energy. The interoceptive analyzers register what is happening inside our body (e.g., where blood is collecting) and communicate these changes to the brain (if a lot of blood is collecting at the extremities of the lower limbs, it means I am standing up). The brain intercepts this information with lightning speed and produces the necessary and desired reactions. Thanks to this complex system, we are able to keep our balance, move our body, and orientate ourselves in space in relation to the plane of the earth (the concepts of above and below are among the principal reference

points for self-orientation, along with the concepts of right
and left, back and forward) and in relation to surrounding
objects. The ability to stay upright and move around and

(*Below*): Center of gravity. From A. Kircher, *Mundus subterraneus,* Amsterdam, Waesberge, 1665. (Courtesy of Biblioteca Trivulziana, Milan.)

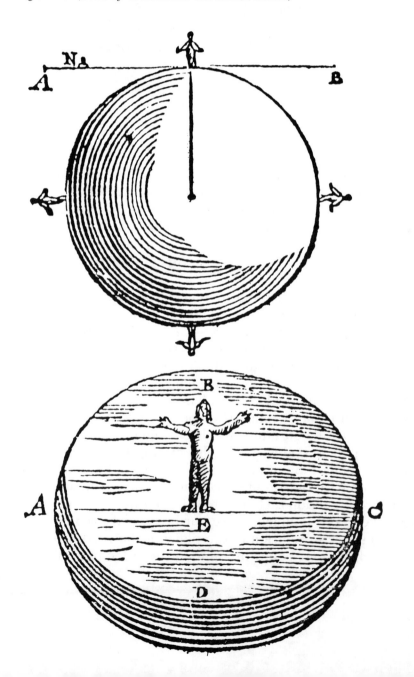

therefore to position our body in relation to the force of gravity—from a hand movement to an acrobatic jump from an Olympic diving board—is an important aspect of our relationship with space.

The Vestibular Apparatus

The force of gravity has literally molded our body (skeleton, muscles, organs) and our perception. This is most ap-

(*Right*): Vestibular apparatus. From Antonio Scarpa, *Anatomica e disquisitiones de audito et olfactu,* Ticini, P. Galetii, 1789. (Courtesy of Biblioteca Comunale, Milan.)

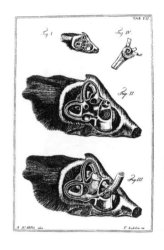

(*Below*): The semicircular canals are located on three mutually perpendicular planes and contain a liquid called endolymph. Their mechanism is connected with the laws of inertia. When the head is held still or is moving in a straight line or uniformly with the body, the endolymph remains immobile, but if the head is turned to one side, the fluid runs in the opposite direction, stimulating the endings of the vestibular nerve. Information about what is happening is transmitted to the brain in the form of nerve impulses. The otolithic apparatus is made up of a tiny follicle at the end of which are sensitive nerve cells with fibers. These are covered in calcium salt crystals bathed in a gelatinous liquid. The force of gravity makes the crystals press on the endings of the vestibular nerve, stimulating it, and the quantity of nervous impulses informs the brain as to the strength of pressure. As is well known, this pressure increases as one descends and decreases as one ascends. It can be felt clearly in mountain areas, in lifts, and during airplane flights. The otolithic apparatus and three semicircular canals. Drawing by Douglas Skene.

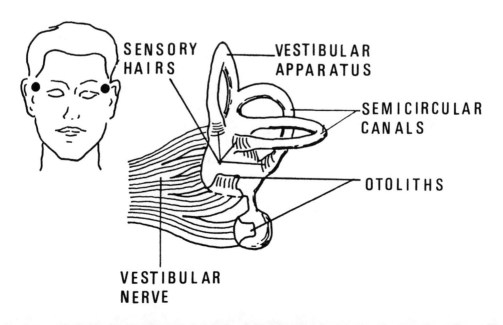

SENSORY HAIRS

VESTIBULAR APPARATUS

SEMICIRCULAR CANALS

OTOLITHS

VESTIBULAR NERVE

parent in the formation and function of one of the principal organs used in the perception of space: the vestibular apparatus. At first sight, it resembles a scale model of the three Cartesian axes, but in fact, it is the three Cartesian axes that are modelled on the shape of this little bone situated on either side of the head, close to the auricular apparatus. The vestibular apparatus does not, like the auricular apparatus, register the vibrations produced by electromagnetic energy, but rather the direction and level of pressure of the force of gravity. It is composed of a sensory apparatus formed by semicircular canals and the otolithic apparatus, which is connected to the brain by means of a bundle of transmitter nerves. According to the physiologist I. F. Tsion, who was the first to describe their function in 1878, the semicircular canals are the peripheral organs of the sense of space. It is thanks to their existence that we are able to form spatial concepts. The otolithic apparatus instead is essentially a sensor of the power of gravity; indeed, it is our body's principal gravity sensor, informing us of every tiny variation that occurs.[18]

Sight, Hearing, and Smell

Leonov and Lebedev make a distinction between orientation in relation to the plane of the earth and orientation in relation to surrounding objects. Orientation in relation to the plane of the earth—which basically regards the way we interact with the force of gravity—is the fundamental component of spatial orientation. It is made possible through the activity of a series of analyzers: the optical analyzer (sight), stato-kinetic analyzer (the vestibular apparatus), proprioceptive analyzer (musculo-articular sensitivity), dermato-mechanical (epidermic sensitivity), and interoceptive analyzers. In order to orient ourselves in relation to objects—and here the term objects should be understood as including all those stimuli originating at some distance from our immediate surroundings—the intervention of other analyzers is required that are capable of intercepting stimuli that are not in direct contact with our body: sight, hearing, and smell. Leonov and Lebedev define

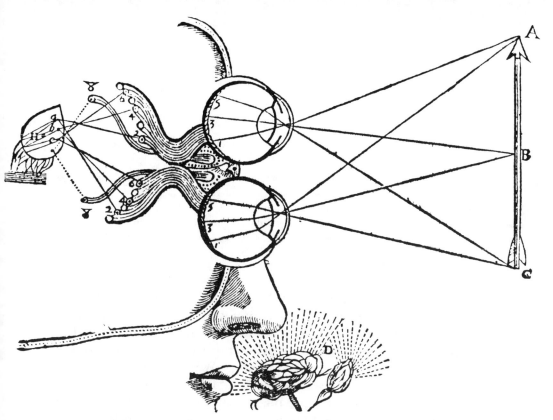

(Above): The image illustrates the Cartesian concept of coordination among the sense organs. According to Descartes, sight takes precedence over smell. The light stimulus coming from ABC causes the corresponding image to be formed on the pineal gland H; the smell stimulus D, on the other hand, attracts no attention. From René Descartes, *L'homme et un traitté de la formation du foetus [. . .] avec les remarques du louys de la forge [. . .] sur le traitté de l'homme de René Descartes, et sur les figures par luy inventées,* Paris, chez Theodore Girard, 1664. (Courtesy of Biblioteca Universitaria, Bologna.)

(Right): Eyeball. From Athanius Kircher, *Ars magna lucis et umbrae,* Athanius Kircher, Rime, apus Hermannum Scheus, 1646. (Courtesy of Biblioteca Trivulziana, Milan.)

these in more precise terms as analyzers that are capable, even from a considerable distance, of differentiating the sources of energy flows.[19] The acoustic and olfactory perception of space basically has the function of locating a sound or smell. Furthermore, they contribute to making the task of perception more pleasant and this has important repercussions, for example, on mnemonic processes. Memory is activated (or totally inhibited) by powerful emotional states. The same happens in the perception of space. It is common to be reminded of certain spaces and certain environments out of all others for their smell.

Sight is a very important sensory analyzer in that it controls large spaces. It is the analyzer with the widest field of

(*Left*): Depiction of the way in which, according to Descartes, the mental image ABCD of the exterior object is formed on the pineal gland H. From René Descartes, *De homine figuris et latinitate donatus a Florentius Schuyl, Lugduni Batavorum*, apud Franciscum Moyardum e Petrum Leffen, 1662. (Courtesy of Biblioteca Comunale Archiginnasio, Bologna.)

action, and the perception of depth is a fundamental aspect of this. It works in close collaboration with the other analyzers, however. The result of this collaboration with the otolithic apparatus, for example, may be seen if we spin round quickly on our feet and then suddenly stop: We experience a visual hallucination that makes us continue for a few seconds to see everything revolving around us. Another example of this is the way certain images—such as a film shot by a telecamera mounted on a fast-moving car—are able to provoke a sense of nausea in the spectator. If we stand upright and move about, it is thanks to the close collaboration of the various analyzers. In fact, we are able to keep our balance and stay upright even with our eyes shut. This feat is made possible by the musculo-articular apparatus, the skin on the soles of our feet (which informs the brain that it is undergoing mechanical energy pressure), and the receptors located in the walls of the blood vessels (which signal that blood is collecting in the lower part of our body). The activity of the various analyzers (both those already mentioned and others as well) is synthesized by certain structures in the cerebral cortex, and this process permits a correct orientation of the body in space.

Subconscious

The bodily functions discussed above are, of course, carried out without our being aware of them. When we are about to lose our balance and fall, the information sent to the brain by the otolith apparatus, musculo-articular apparatus, and other receptors that counter the force of gravity with the body mass allows us to regain our balance automatically. Since they are automatic functions, it is physiologically not necessary to

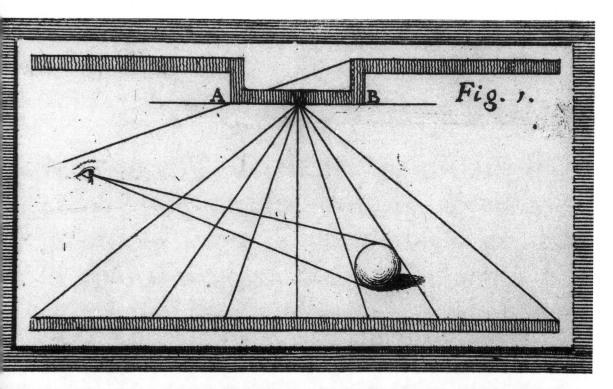

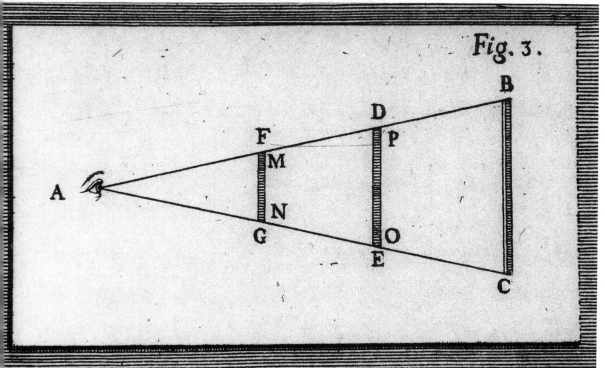

Studies of depth perception. From Leonardo da Vinci, *Trattato della pittura di Leonardo da Vinci nuovamente dato in luce con la vita dell'autore stesso scritta da Raffael du Fresne*, Bologna, Istituto delle Scienze, 1786. (Courtesy of Biblioteca Comunale, Milan.)

Seventeenth century frescos depicting loggias, niches, windows, and lunettes, Dome of the Chiesa dell'Incoronata, Sabbioneta, Italy. (Courtesy of Soprintendenza per i Beni Artistici e Storici di Mantova.)

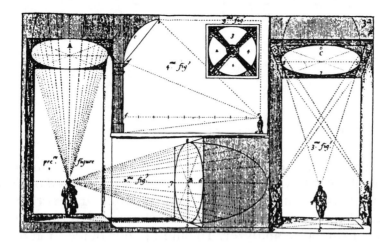

be aware of them. This allows the brain to use its conscious part for other activities. It is only necessary to make a rational analysis of automatic processes when there is a dysfunction and the mechanism breaks down for some reason. It is not particularly interesting to open the hood of a car and tinker with the engine, batteries, and spark plugs: It is a task one only undertakes if there is something wrong. Or in our case, if the engine has not broken down, but is making a funny noise.

The Perception of Depth

We perceive the shape, dimensions, and movement of an object and other features of its surface through the controlled

(*Above*): Perspective-based representation techniques. From Abraham Bosse, *Maniere universelle de Mr. Desargues pour pratiquer la perspective*, Paris, 1648. (Courtesy of Donatella Ravizza.)

(*Below*): Galleria degli Antichi, Palazzo Giardino, Sabbloneta, Italy. (Courtesy of Sovrintendenza per i Beni Artistici e Storici di Mantova.)

activity of a number of functions. We cannot determine its dimensions solely on the basis of the image projected onto our retina; this requires instead a coordinated interaction between the retina and eye muscles, the sensitive and motor areas of the optic analyzer. To sum up, our perception of the

Perspective-based drawing. From Jacopo Barozzi (Vignola), *Le due regole della prospettiva pratica coi commenti di l Danti,* Rome, Mascardi Printing House, 1644. (Courtesy of Biblioteca Comunale, Milan.)

distance, volume, size, and shape of objects is achieved on the basis of a series of data and by means of certain processes: the size of the image on the retina, the tension of the eye muscles, accommodation (the ability of the eye to control the quantity of light entering it and the sensitivity of the retina), convergence (the modification of the lens in order to focus light on the retina), and the nonidentical nature of the right-hand and left-hand images. Studies have shown that the maximum range for accommodation is 25 meters, whereas for convergence it is 300 to 350 meters.[20] Beyond these limits, the perception of size and recession is based on indirect signals such as a comparison with other objects, the dimensions of which are known, or sharpness of outline.

The perception of depth is important at both a physiological and psychological level. Research conducted during missions to outer space has demonstrated that the absence of visual reference points in an environment results in a tendency to short-sightedness, for the eyes are only able to focus on objects very near at hand. The ability to evaluate distance is also lost. It would thus appear that being able to focus on infinity maintains our visual system in good order. However, this is not the only benefit. The perception of depth is important for our mental life, just as the perception of a wide variety of sensory stimuli is important for maintaining healthy cerebral activity. It is interesting in this context to cite the results of a study carried out on a group of African children who from an early age had been carried on their mothers' backs in a sling. The perception of a very limited space ending at their mothers' shoulders, the obstruction of the view of the landscape, and the impossibility of seeing the environments and spaces being traversed resulted in an intellectual activity which was inferior to that of children carried in the arms or a carriage or stroller. Perceiving depth means being able to think in terms of the relations that exist between the things that one sees, and this, because it requires complex thought processes, produces a high level of mental stimulation.

Interestingly, even the representation of a space is sufficient to allow the brain to perceive depth. Painters and architects have always tried to give the illusion of depth to things
that are in reality flat, the illusion of openness to what in
reality is closed (and here we might recall the famous tromp
l'oeil by Padre Pozzo painted on the ceiling of the Church of

(*Facing page top*): Sala delle Muse, frescos by Battista del Moro, Villa Godi-Malinverni,
Lonedo, Italy, 1540. Architect: Andrea Palladio. (Courtesy of the Malinverni family.)

(*Below and facing page bottom*): Interior views, Villa Godi-Malinverni, Lonedo, Italy, 1540.
Architect: Andrea Palladio. (Courtesy of the Malinverni family.)

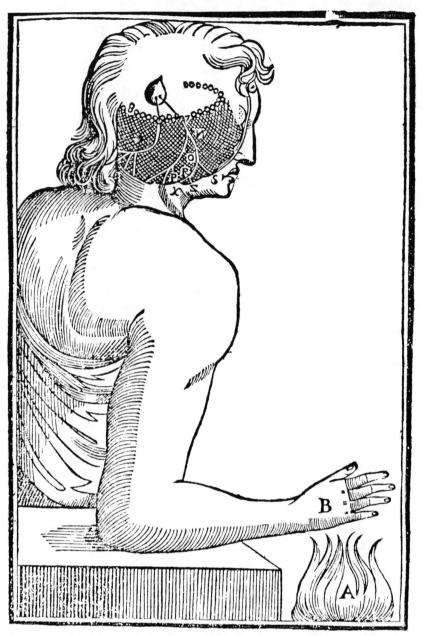

Depiction of the automatic impulse by which a hand is withdrawn when burned, according to Descartes. From René Descartes, *L'homme et un traitté de la formation du foetus [. . .] avec les remaques du louys de la forge [. . .] sur le traitté de l'homme de René Descartes, e sur les figures par luy inventees*, Paris, chez Theodore Girard, 1664. (Courtesy of Biblioteca Universitaria, Bologna.)

Sant'Ignazio in Rome). Tromp l'oeil work has always been admired for the great technical skill it displayed. It is now also recognized as something that fulfills a physiological and psychological need (this is why psychologists working in space agencies recommend the use of photographs and mirrors in spacecraft interiors).

Seeing by Touch

According to Bechterev, the fundamental elements of spatial vision are knowing how to maintain an upright position and the sensations that come from an exploring hand and investigative eye. In short, spatial vision is determined by a complex series of vestibular-visual-stato-kinetic sensations.[21] It is in part based, therefore, on the experience of touch. Looking at an object is a very similar sensation to touching it. In a certain sense, the hand reproduces an object as it touches it, registering its shape, size, and characteristics. By means of impulses transmitted by the motor apparatus, the brain is able to formulate a copy of it. The automatic connection between touching and seeing—between hand and eye movements—is made during infancy. Later, we learn to link the visual sensation to the tactile one without having to touch. Tactile perception does not simply involve the hands. We perceive space and the objects in our surroundings like a sort of extension of our body. It is as if we transpired not only through our skin, but through our clothes and the surrounding walls as well. We touch or rather we feel surfaces that are close to us. The importance of epidermic feeling in perceiving space is apparent in the problems our body encounters when subjected to long periods in hypostimulatory environments. "Sensory starvation" is an important topic of research for the research centers of space agencies, since it is a condition typical of confined and highly technological environments.

What we define as *the perception of space* is the synthesis of the activity of a number of analyzers and structures located in the cerebral cortex triggered by a series of outside stimuli. Each analyzer registers a part or an aspect of the complex stimulus that we perceive as a unitary whole and identify as space. As Lebedev and Leonov emphasize, the combined activity of the several analyzers that form a so-called functional

One of the first designs for the space station Freedom. In the foreground, the European laboratory, Columbus. (Courtesy of Alenia Spazio.)

system is superior to the activity of each single component. This combined activity allows us to respond to a multiple stimulus with a global reaction rather than single, separate reactions. This is the most effective and complete form of behavior for a body in relation to the external medium.[22]

Mutants

This complex apparatus is adapted to work perfectly on earth, but it is extraordinary to watch its behavior when, as happens in outer space, it registers unfamiliar stimuli. In an environment without gravity, the otolithic apparatus is not very useful: In such situations, greater importance is assumed by the other sensorial analyzers. On leaving the space module in his spacesuit, an astronaut can only move about if he has developed certain abilities. He must use his perceptual system differently. In fact, the nerve impulses coming from the musculo-articular apparatus and the skin do not allow him to develop concepts about the spatial relationship between his body and the objects surrounding him. He receives stimuli regarding the interrelationships between the various parts of his body. Consequently, outside the spaceship, the astronaut cannot orientate himself by means of the visual, tactile, and musculo-articular sensations he receives: He has to learn how to orientate himself on the basis of his visual perception alone. Our body can also adapt itself to conditions that are very different from those characterizing the earth's environment. It can even learn to orientate itself in outer space. However, it can do this only if it is able to establish new relationships between the sense organs. The sensory system has to adapt to new stimuli by modulating its analyzers differently, in a process similar to the refinement of the senses of touch and hearing in the blind. The body becomes so accustomed to this new environment that, on landing back on earth after a long voyage, astronauts are almost incapable of walking.

Even on earth, however, we live inside casings that demand particular abilities of our organism: automobiles, for example. It would be interesting to discover what sort of changes are taking place in our perceptual system as a result of spending so much time in these vehicles, as well as in highly technological and artificial environments, characterized by elements such as artificial light and air, synthetic materials, colors with certain saturation and value levels, geometrical spatial configurations, small dimensions, etc.

THE PSYCHOLOGICAL LEVEL

The Affective Dimension

We become aware of the existence of an emotional bond with space only when it breaks for some reason and pain is experienced as a result. Moving house or relocating is not at all the innocuous phenomenon we are led to believe it is. The problem does not simply concern the physical exertion of packing and transporting furniture or objects: It involves a highly traumatic psychic and emotional exertion for the human body as well.

Information on the existence of "human roots" comes from studies carried out in the 1970s by researchers in environmental perception based at the City University of New York.[23] Basically, what these studies showed was that a very special and important bond is formed between human beings and spaces, above all in two delicate phases of life: childhood and old age. In both these periods, in fact, albeit for different reasons, the human body requires a stable physical setting. The process of abandoning one's own physical setting and adapting to a new one is traumatic for everybody, but especially difficult for an elderly person. The aging process causes a weakening of the body's basic faculties and the functions by which it relates to the environment—such as sensory acuteness and motor ability—with a consequent increase in problems concerning external control. For young children too, moving to unfamiliar territory is a serious problem. Children need a stable, familiar, secure environment in order for them to learn and develop their potential and abilities to the fullest. It is important for human beings to feel, during infancy, that they belong to a place and to establish with that place a relationship of positive, reciprocal interdependence. They are then able to move competently in the various environments of everyday adult life.

Humans (and animals too) need to put down roots in the places they inhabit, just as plants do. These roots are not of the physical type that anchor one's feet materially to the soil, but are rather invisible, impalpable structures that sink deep down into our emotions, feelings, and mental makeup. When such roots fail to develop in a person, serious mental unbalance may result, whereas in the case of "weak" individuals, sudden uprooting is liable to provoke internal wounds that can even result in death.

After the difficult childhood years, roots allow the human organism to go through periods of nomadism before returning to a phase in which it once again needs to have a fixed and permanent sense of place.

An appreciation of the affective component in the space–human-organism relationship is of the utmost importance in the design of places for people in childhood and old age: Making adequate provision for this would allow us to avoid the serious errors that blindness caused by ignorance often prevents us from seeing.

Spatial Identity

The act of sinking one's roots into a space allows one to form what Harold Proshansky calls a spatial identity and defines as a substructure of one's personal identity. The development of a meaningful spatial identity is dependent on there being consistency and continuity in one's first steps toward discovery of the physical environment and directly influences the growth of one's personal identity. If one's spatial identity is distorted, the completion of one's personal identity is threatened. Spatial identity is developed during the child's very first experiences of socialization and manifests itself as a strong attachment to a place (it is stronger in some people than others).

However, spatial identity is a cognitive structure, the complexity of which goes far beyond a simple emotional attachment to a particular place. It consists of a series of notions about the physical environment that serve to define, maintain, and protect one's personal identity. These notions have to do with knowing and being able to move around and make use of the physical-social environments of which one becomes a part. The spatial categories of privacy, personal space, overcrowding, and territoriality play an important part in this. Spatial identity is also of fundamental importance as a parameter for design, yet it is for the most part still ignored. Architects—or those who work with space usually know, at the intuitive level, the existence of this dimension of the human space–body relationship. But as we have seen, an intuitive approach to the design of highly artificial environments is not sufficient.

Perception of the Environment

Space (as a physical component of an environment) has the power to condition behavior and form personality. Without resorting to the extremes of the behavioral psychologists, for whom the human being is simply a product of the external environment, we can say that the environment affects—at times very powerfully—our emotions, feelings, and reactions. We establish a psychological as well as a sensorial relationship with the environment, both in a physical and social sense (though naturally, it is with the social sense that environmental psychologists are most concerned). According to some researchers, we are far more attentive to the information transmitted by the environment than any other type of data. People make decisions, sometimes irreversible decisions, about environments before they even enter them, and this makes them see environments in a preconstituted way. At the same time, however, the environment itself also exerts an influence and in certain situations this can be very strong.

William Ittelson has formulated a series of hypotheses regarding the way in which people perceive and react to stimuli-information coming from the environment. His essay ends with the hope that further studies will develop his hypotheses more fully. It is a hope that has not yet been realized.[24]

Another researcher who has contributed to the study of the environment—conceived not as a chaotic and casual series of stimuli, but as a system regulated by precise laws—is Roger Barker. According to Barker, people usually accept the laws of the environment. If one behaves in a way that strays too far from the behavior required in a given setting, one risks reproof or even expulsion (as will be proved if one tries to dance in a church or sing in a courtroom). This is why people generally respond in a positive way to the behavioral requirements of a given environment. The environment therefore conditions behavior. Responses are naturally of an individual nature. In the case of children, Barker states that 75 percent show a positive response to environmental requirements. We now know, in fact, that space has great manipulative power over children, and that it is a fundamental element in the formation of personality and personal identity.[25]

Ittelson's studies, like those of Barker, come to the conclusion that there is a very strong relationship between people and the environment. The fact has to be emphasized that designing an environment, both in the physical and social sense (the two are anyway inextricably linked together), means provoking reactions in people (that are more or less predetermined) and affecting their personalities.

The Symbolic Dimension

When we talk about such architectural masterpieces as the pyramids, the Colosseum, gothic cathedrals, and St. Peter's Basilica, we are referring above all to their symbolic dimension. By this is meant the ability of space to communicate with deep dimensions of our ego, or rather, our ability to represent and see outside of ourselves and in spatial structures, profound and important parts of our personality.

Much has been written about the symbolic dimension of architecture (and I leave it to the reader to consult the relevant publications). Here, I want simply to make the observation that it is possible to speak of a symbolic dimension above-all in relation to classical architecture. It is much more difficult to do so with contemporary architecture. Classical architecture had a language, a precise grammar, and its own rules. Though this language undoubtedly served to communicate the way of thinking of a ruling class, it did so by means of a "discourse." The ability to communicate through architectural forms today seems diminished, yet it is this ability that permits architecture to enter the world of art. For in addition to power, artists also use the architectural form to "speak."

The tower of the Ducal Palace, Urbino, Italy. (Photo: Douglas Skene.)

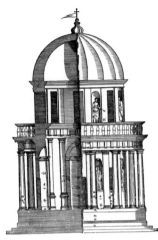

(*Left*): View of San Pietro in Montorio. From Andrea Palladio, *l quattro libri dell'architettura*, Venice, Carampello, 1581. (Courtesy of Biblioteca Trivulziana, Milan.)

(*Below*): Section of the Pantheon. From Andrea Palladio, *l quattro libri dell'architettura*, Venice, Carampello, 1581. (Courtesy of Biblioteca Trivulziana, Milan.)

(*Facing page right*): Interior of Milan Cathedral, Milan, Italy. (Photo: Donatella Ravizza.)

The Cultural Dimension (America and Italy)

In a brief note to his famous *The Hidden Dimension,* the anthropologist Edward T. Hall states that the way in which an organism perceives an environment depends on four factors: his status, activity, the setting, and experience. To these may be added a further, often ignored factor: culture.[26] All over the industrialized world, environments are being designed and built for housing offices, fastfood restaurants, shopping malls, etc. They are exact models of prototypes developed in the United States on the basis of needs, desires, and strategies peculiar to North American culture. However, to state that cultures differ from one another means stating that there are different ways of perceiving space, moving, expressing oneself, speaking, organizing one's time, reacting to situations, being with other people, eating, and thinking.

It is exceedingly difficult to analyze Italian cultural characteristics due to the lack of documentation on the subject. This reluctance to adopt a scientific approach in cataloguing certain aspects of life usually left to the mercy of intuition is in itself indicative of the Italian approach. Broadly speaking, we could be said to differ from North Americans on two counts: our way of communicating and our way of using time (which consequently bears a relation to the use we make of space). As far as communication is concerned, Hall draws a line between highly or weakly contextualized cultures. In the first case, information is highly contextualized and interiorized in the people. In the second, the bulk of information content is to be found explicitly in the message (the method of communication between two twins who have grown up together is of a type considered strongly contextualized; that of two lawyers in court is weakly contextualized). America, Germany, and Switzerland could be said to constitute weakly contextualized cultures. Interpersonal communication in a high context culture is of maximum importance. Italy undoubtedly belongs to the first group.

Another way in which the two systems differ markedly is their way of perceiving and organizing time. Broadly speaking, events in North America are considered separately and sequentially (monochronic time), whereas in Mediterranean culture, such events coexist simultaneously (polychronic time). Organizing one's time in a polychronic manner means also attributing importance to the involvement of people with the process. A monochronic culture is more directed toward achieving objectives; a polychronic culture on the other hand has a greater propensity toward human relations and the family, which constitutes its real *raison d'etre*. Here, one is dealing with two very different ways of communicating and organizing time. Both obviously work, although Hall emphasizes the importance of not imposing one system on people that belong to the other cultural group.

Hypothetical space colony of the twenty-first century. (Courtesy of NASA.)

The SIVRA simulation laboratory lit by warm and cold light. Vertical lamps are used for studying possible ways of simulating light apertures in the walls. SIVRA Laboratory, IGuzzini Illuminazione, Recanati, Italy, 1992. Architects: Piera Scuri, Douglas Skene, and Daniele Bedini. The following companies took part in the project: Sadi, Oece, Unifor, and Bardelli. (Courtesy of IGuzzini Illuminazione.)

The SIVRA simulation laboratory *(continued)*.

The SIVRA simulation laboratory *(continued)*.

View of entrance. SIVRA Laboratory, scale model. (Photo: Douglas Skene.)

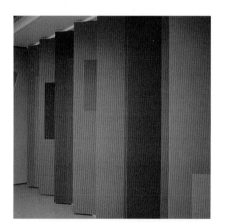

The colored panels are painted on either side with warm and cold colors, allowing the color temperature of the laboratory to be studied. They are finished with Oece "peach skin" paint. SIVRA Laboratory, IGuzzini Illuminazione, Recanati, Italy, 1992. Architects: Piera Scuri, Douglas Skene, and Daniele Bedini. (Courtesy of IGuzzini Illuminazione.)

Sketches for the SIVRA laboratory entrance. Drawing by Douglas Skene.

Walls, Edinburgh Castle. (Photo: Piera Scuri.)

Following spread
Background: Industrial plant background.
Left: Control room, Himont Italia, Ferrara, Italy, 1989. Architects: Piera Scuri and Douglas Skene. (Photo: Dida Biggi.)
Right: Control room, Enichem Elastomeri, Ferrara, Italy, 1990. Architects: Piera Scuri and Douglas Skene. (Photo: Dida Biggi.)

Corridor, control room, Enichem Elastomeri, Ferrara, Italy, 1990. Architects: Piera Scuri and Douglas Skene. (Photo: Dida Biggi.)

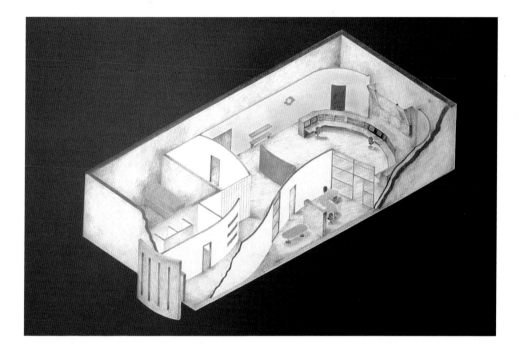

Control room, Enichem Elastomeri, Ferrara, Italy, 1990. Architects: Piera Scuri and Douglas Skene. Axonometric and rendering.

Control room, Enichem Elastomeri, Ravenna, Italy, 1992. Architects: Piera Scuri and Douglas Skene. Rendering by Temma Katsuya.

Monte Cassiano, Italy. (Photo: Piera Scuri.)

The "artificial skylight," or dynamic lighting system, has been tested at the Lighting Research Center of the Rensselaer Polytechnic Institute in Troy, New York. Statistical analysis of data showed that the daylight simulating skylight can be used to improve the mood and performance of night shift workers on complex cognitive tasks.

Medieval town in Umbria. (Photo: Douglas Skene.)

As far as the American working environment is concerned, the American office (which along with shopping centers is being mass-imported to Italy) has a homogeneous spatial layout that hardly appears to differ from Alaska to Florida, involving reception areas, lobbies, general offices, meeting rooms, executive offices, boardrooms, cafeterias, diningrooms, waiting areas, etc. Hall speaks quite explicitly of the importance that standardization and uniformity have for the American way of life.[27] This fact has its spatial equivalent in the division of cities into virtually identical-looking blocks. American production techniques and technical capabilities

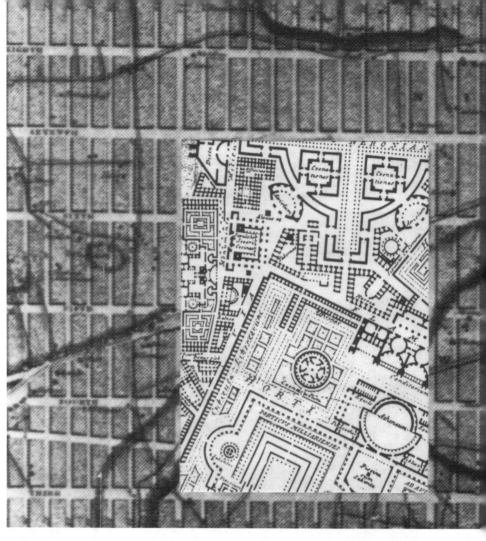

Grid of Manhattan's plan and a fragment of "Campo Marzio dell'antica Roma" engraved by Piranesi.

are based on deep-rooted cultural characteristics. Italy is quite obviously another matter, where entering an office one is not familiar with often constitutes a veritable adventure. Offices with very different characteristics may be found within the same city, not to mention the difference that might exist between an office in Milan and one in Naples, between a public and privately owned office, that of a family business and one clearly organized along North American lines. Italian individualism on the other hand is well known (hundreds of dialects bear witness to this on a linguistic level). This individualism in its worst form makes it difficult for Italians to work as a team, something that in the United States is a simple matter of course.

It is no secret that Italians have a rather low opinion of open space planning. The preferred spatial divide in Italy is the room, even if overcrowded. But what is the significance of a room from a sensory point of view? Basically, it is a relatively small space surrounded by walls with one or more windows and doors. In other words, to be in a room means having the wall, the door, and the window a few meters away. It means using all the stimuli (sensorial and mental) that these elements produce. In an open office plan especially in a central position where work stations are often situated, the wall tends to recede into the background, and one loses all perception of it. The same may be said of the windows and doors. On a sensory level, one loses contact with the divide that separates the individual from the outside world, the "wall," but also with the window seen as a threshold representing the divide between inside and outside, in itself an important source of sensory stimulus. As we know, mental activity diminishes with the lessening of sensory stimuli. Furthermore, the distant location of the divide (the external wall) appears to be felt as a loss of contact with reality and raises the level of abstraction (a fact of no small importance in a space where the vast majority of people work with computers). The central internal position of a large space, even when some protection is offered by panels, can create a sense of insecurity, whereas three or four people working in a room (despite the total lack of visual and acoustic privacy that this situation affords) can give reassurance (the panel does not seem to be perceived as a limit or border, but more as a screen and hence as such precarious). Unlike the walls, it does not "communicate" messages of solidity and security. Perhaps it is easier for people accustomed to contact with others and human relations to isolate themselves by constructing mental barriers and not using partitions and screens. Consequently, the room as opposed to open space constitutes a radically different spatial solution.

This cultural difference also involves the sphere of sensory perception. We perceive the space and objects that surround us as a sort of extension of our bodies. In a certain sense, we transpire through our skin but also through our

(Right and facing page): Window study by Vignola. From P. Letarouilly, *Edifices de Rome moderne*, Liege, D'Avanzo, 1853. (Courtesy of Biblioteca d'Arte, Castello Sforzesco, Milan.)

clothes and the surrounding walls. Furthermore, we "touch" or at least "feel" the surfaces close to us. Here also the cultural factor comes into play because our skin (and our brain) is not used to surroundings made of glass, aluminum, or plastic. Our skin, as far as constructed space is concerned, is accustomed to bricks, stones, and rocks. Metal walls covered with laminated plastic and in the best cases with fabric or wood give rise to environments in which it is particularly difficult to "breathe."

Thus, the cultural viewpoint provides us with important information regarding the intensity and type of sensory stimulation that must be possessed by an environment. Contrary to North American and North European culture, Mediterranean culture surrounds itself with sensory worlds that are very much more alive.

In the United States, the hierarchical structure and reigning philosophy within multinationals have been the principal influences on the design of office space. The power that typifies the multinationals is there for all to see (there are numerous instances of American politicians being hounded out of office for having hidden or denied events connected to their personal

lives). Within working environments, social hierarchy is clearly signalled by space and furnishings: A relative amount of space corresponds to a relative amount of power. Hence, space immediately maps out a person's role inside the organization (the secretary's area, general and management offices, cafeteria and executive dining rooms, conference rooms, and boardrooms). In the American office, the chairperson or president will certainly occupy the largest and most beautiful room with the most windows situated on the highest floor of the building. Power in Italy takes on manifestly different forms. In order to understand the type of social relationship that results, one must appreciate the importance of the family in Italian society generally, and in Italian businesses in particular (even at the management level). Unlike American working environments, Italian environments do not openly reflect the social hierarchy, or at least not in the same way. In Italy, power tends to be more concealed than revealed. In casting a cursory glance inside an Italian office, it can at times be difficult to establish who the boss is.

The surroundings are slightly less defined here, we could say more ambiguous. In Italy, managers (whether men or women) are quite likely to work behind desks-similar in most respects to those of their direct subordinates. People tend to hide rather than reveal their roles (in the same way, certain severe and imposing buildings in Milan conceal hidden treasures in the form of luxurious gardens and cloisters). Introducing an American spatial system thus entails confronting a not inconsiderable series of communication problems.

In the planning of highly artificial environments, very close attention should be given to the cultural aspect. In fact, to ignore cultural norms means forcing people to live and behave in an unnatural way: It is (to use an architectural metaphor) like building staircases in places that are destined for people with no legs.

The Emotional Dimension

Our first, immediate reaction to our surroundings is of an emotional nature. In the space of a few seconds, our emotions allow us to form an idea, or more precisely, an impression, of the surrounding environment.

Naturally, the emotional response is extremely subjective, varying from person to person. In this context, the experiences recorded by Glavcosomos researchers are enlightening: Lebedev and Leonov describe the different reactions of a group of pilots during an experiment carried out in a state of weightlessness. Being in a state of weightlessness does not simply mean floating pleasantly in the air. It also means that our body—the otolithic apparatus first and foremost—starts to receive an enormous number of unfamiliar stimuli. Fundamental reference points such as "above" and "below" no longer exist and this can cause a profound sense of disorientation. It thus becomes difficult for the brain to give appropriate orders to the legs and arms in order to move.

The diverse nature of emotional reactions was such that the subjects taking part in the experiment were divided into three groups. In the first group were those able to maintain a good capacity for work, despite the fact that the absence of gravity had turned their environmental conditions literally upside down. Indeed, these subjects were found to be pleasantly surprised by the sensation of extreme lightness (among them, naturally, was Yuri Gagarin). The second group instead reacted with feelings of disorientation and frequently reported sensations such as falling and not knowing whether to turn right or left. Some pilots entered a state of euphoria and became so excited that they were unable to complete their work, engaging in play instead. Others had visual hallucinations accompanied by unpleasant sensations of anguish and insecurity. These reactions then disappeared once the subjects became accustomed to their new state. The third group reacted very badly both psychologically and physically: They suffered nausea, feelings of horror and fear, especially of falling. In these cases, the disorientation was total and accompanied by a strong sense of isolation, headache, and dizziness. Researchers called this complex of negative reactions the "world destruction syndrome." The astronaut Shmar'yan describes how, terrified, he felt himself falling and saw the space inside the cockpit grow larger and then suddenly smaller. Everything seemed to him to be strange and unrecognizable; he thought he saw trees in the distance being uprooted, volcanos erupting, the earth laid waste, and he believed himself to be dying. These sensations lasted for one to two minutes. The same symptoms appear, according to psychologists, in some neuro-psychotics when one of the symptoms of their illness is the sense of weightlessness.[28]

We can therefore see that there are different emotional reactions to strong stimuli coming from the surrounding environment. In fact, the absence of gravity is a very unusual stimulus. It may be received without unleashing sensations of panic only by people with a sound nervous system who are able to receive novel information with positive emotions. This makes us think of some observations made by Bruno Zevi on the subject of the often negative reactions aroused by truly new architectural works. And of the difficulty human beings have, especially some of them, in accepting "the new."[29]

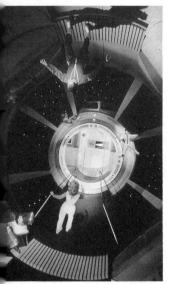

Hypothetical extraterrestial house, Epcot Center, Disneyworld, Orlando, Florida. (Photo: Dida Biggi.)

Astronauts in microgravity: image elaborated on computer by Douglas Skene.

THE NATURALIZATION
OF ARTIFICIAL ENVIRONMENTS

What is the purpose of gaining an understanding of the physiological, psychic, or emotional dimension of the perception of space? It may be used in order to understand what kind of influence a space, in its various aspects, can exert on our life and our body and the way in which it should therefore be designed. We know on the basis of the physiological dimension of the perception of space that to live in a given environment not only conditions behavior, but also influences our psychic structure (most important during infancy) and sensorial world. In addition, it influences the way we perceive and stimulates to a greater or lesser degree our brain, thus influencing our psychological state. In a highly artificial environment in which almost everything that surrounds us has been created by human beings, such knowledge is essential. It makes it possible to reproduce certain aspects of nature (air and light, e.g.) in a way that is artificial yet appropriate, or, that is, in a way that is not harmful to health, either from a psychological or physiological point of view. It may also protect our nature (and culture) from artificial dimensions.

As we have already stated, space constitutes an extraordinarily rich source of stimuli and information that are intercepted by the sense organs and elaborated by the higher nervous centers. This process contributes to producing human sensations and reactions. If the relationship that binds us to space is basically a kind of communicative system (an exchange, a passage of energy), it is

"Internal and external senses." From Juan Komensky, *Joh. amos comenii orbis sensualium pictus quadrilinguis, hoc est, omnium fundamentalium in mundo rerum, et in vita actionum, pictura et nomenclatura, Germanica, Latina, Italica, et Gallica. Cum titolorum juxta, atque vocabolarum indice,* Nuremberg, M. Endteri, 1658. (Courtesy of Biblioteca Nazionale Centrale, Florence.)

(*Right*): Eyeball. From Jacopo Barozzi (Vignola), *Le due regole della prospettiva pratica coi comment di I. Danti*, Rome, Mascardi Printing House, 1644. (Courtesy of Biblioteca Comunale, Milan.)

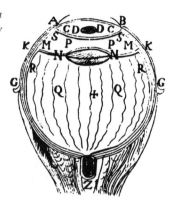

The automatic impulse by which a hand is withdrawn when burned, according to Descartes. From René Descartes, *De homine figuris et latinitate donatus a Florentius Schuyl, Lugduni Batavorum*, apud Franciscum Moyardum e Petrum Leffen, 1662. (Courtesy of Biblioteca Archiginnasio Bologna.)

important to evaluate the working conditions of the transmitting and receiving poles. The problem therefore regards both the perceptual apparatus and superior nerve centers of contemporary human beings, as well as the condition of environments.

As far as the perceptual apparatus is concerned, it seems that contemporary human beings have difficulty in correctly perceiving space and time. In his book, *Il linguaggio moderno dell'architettura,* Bruno Zevi writes that in the course of civilization, man has lost certain essential values, and among these is space-time unity.[30] Space-time unity, to use Zevi's term, means simply a harmonious living dimension. It is precisely this displacement, this complicated integration in today's lifestyle, that causes the malfunctioning of our perceptual apparatus. Since it is built by contemporary human beings, the planned (artificial) environment carries in its forms the space-time distortions that have been described above. A sort of vicious circle thus forms, for there is a reciprocal interrelation between human beings and the environment: Just as man manipulates the external environment, it also manipulates him.

Knowledge about the binding relationship between the human body and space might contribute to lessening our confusion, and it might also improve the quality of the environments in which we live. It would suffice to design them in such a way that made allowance for the efficient working of human perception. (In the same way, spaceship design attempts to compensate for a perceptual apparatus unsuited to the physical conditions of outer space. The design of a space capsule interior is based also on the emotions and perceptions that the pilot will experience during the space flight, the aim being to preserve life and enhance work capacity. The cognitive, physiological, and sensorial aspects of the perception of space are particularly studied.) Perfecting the design of spaces that allow for a healthy sensorial life is no longer the exclusive prov-

(*Facing page*): One of the four clocks on the Metropolitan Life Tower, New York, 1909.

ince of extreme environments. It is a problem that concerns many of the environments we encounter in our everyday life. We pass many hours of the day in closed and highly artificial environments that, though often technologically advanced, are rarely designed for our well-being.

Clock mechanism, De Plano
offices, New York, 1989. Architect: Sandro Marpillero.
(Courtesy of Sandro Marpillero.)

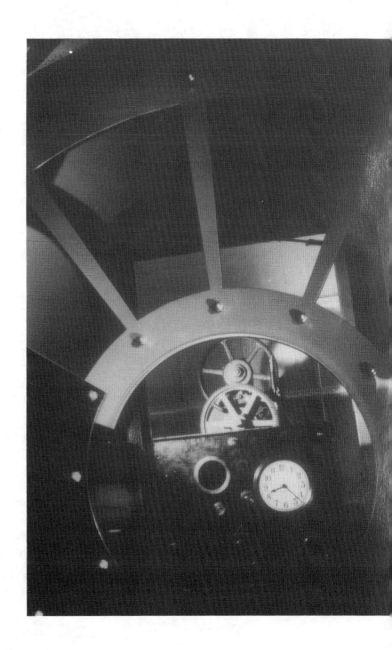

The sunflower. From Athanius Kircher, *Magnes sive de magnetica arte*, Roma, apud Hermannum Scheus, 1641. (Courtesy of Biblioteca Trivulziana, Milan.)

102

CHAPTER 4

THE PERCEPTION OF LIGHT AND COLOR

Lighting the Body

During the course of evolution, the human organism has adapted physiologically to the periodic geophysical and meteorological changes caused by the earth's rotation around its

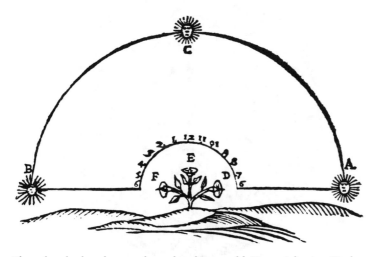

The solar rhythm that regulates the plant world. From Athanius Kircher, *Magnes sive de magnetica arte,* Rome, apud Hermannum Scheus, 1641. (Courtesy of Biblioteca Trivulziana, Milan.)

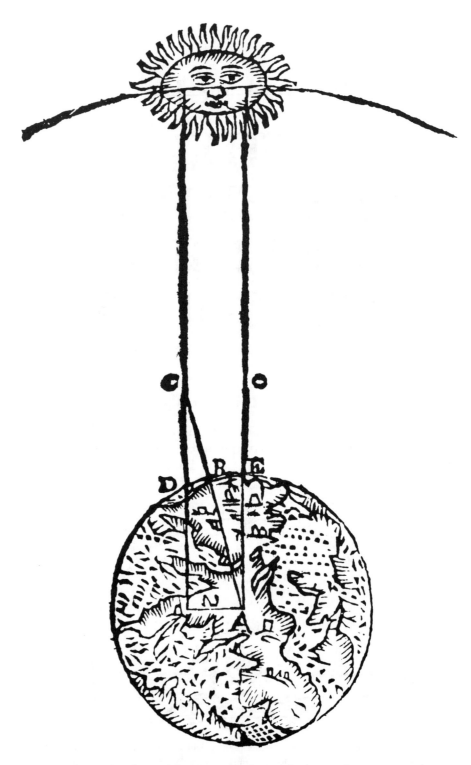

The incidence of sunbeams falling on earth. From Athanius Kircher, *Ars magna lucis et umbrae*, Rome, apud Hermannum Scheus, 1646. (Courtesy of Biblioteca Trivulziana, Milan.)

axis and the sun. The sleep-wake rhythm, variations in body temperature, pulse, respiration, and metabolic rates, and the other physiological functions that slow down during the night, are the product of the body's adaptation to the geophysical phenomena characterizing the earth's environment (the light-

The illumination of the earth and rhythm of the seasons. From Athanius Kircher, *Ars magna lucis et umbrae*, Rome, apud Hermannum Scheus, 1646. (Courtesy of Biblioteca Trivulziana, Milan.)

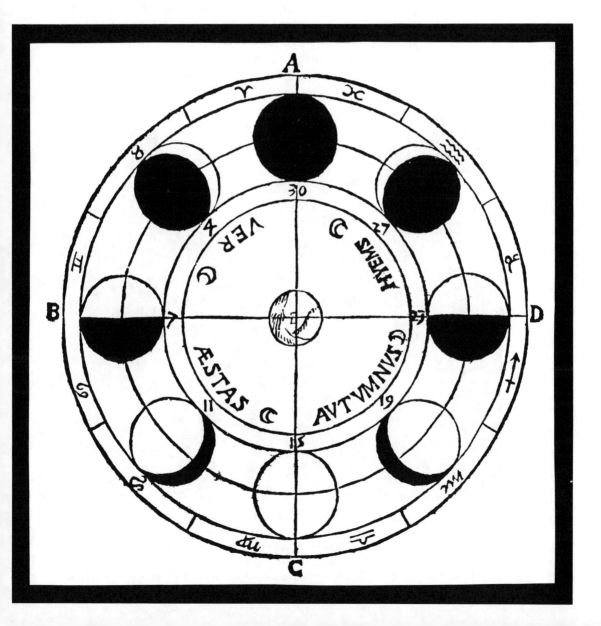

dark cycle, daytime increase in temperature and cosmic radiation, the nighttime drop in humidity and barometric pressure, the changing seasons, etc.). Our organism is both a "rhythmical system" (the way in which we walk, breathe, blink, eat, and sleep is rhythmic) and an "open system," whose equilibrium is maintained by genetic factors (pacemakers) and environmental elements of a geophysical and social type (synchronizers). In other words, our biological clock is not automatic. It has to be regulated every day by synchronizers and especially by the most important synchronizer of all: light.

In both the commerce and service sectors, there are many work environments that are totally devoid of natural light. Offices, supermarkets, large department stores, and shops are all lit exclusively by artificial light, and this is not only true of

"Skybridges" in Anchorage, Alaska. As a result of the harsh climate, closed passageways are widespread. It is possible to leave the house in the morning, drive the car to work, do the shopping, and return home without ever going outside. Large quantities of glass are used despite the lack of insulation this material offers. Such is the need for light in the winter months that the problems of energy consumption take second place. (Photo: Dida Biggi.)

large cities. Without going into the reasons that have brought about this transformation, let us consider what it actually means to live in environments that are lit exclusively by artificial light. Research carried out in confined environments has provided some useful data on this subject. It should, however, be borne in mind that although these experiments required individuals to spend long periods of time inside confined environments without any contact whatsoever with natural light, such conditions differ somewhat from those experienced by an office worker, e.g., who goes home every evening and has the weekend off. But at the same time, the office worker may keep up this lifestyle for many years, so that in the end, the total amount of time he spends inside an artificially lit environment, although not continuous, is enormous.

Light does not just serve to see with; it is also one of the principal environmental synchronizers used by our organism to maintain its equilibrium. Light regulates the sleep-wake cycle. And although it is true that we have a biological time cycle, it is also true that without the help of environmental synchronizers, this cycle goes out of phase. The very close bond between the body and its environment is thus evident.

The importance of light on a psycho-neuro-endocrinal level has been shown by both photobiology and research conducted in confined environments. Knowledge of this sort has a special relevance for the planning of environments that are to be lit wholly by artificial light. In such cases, the purpose of artificial light is no longer to complement and thus extend natural light, but rather to substitute for it altogether. In photobiological terms, we might say that artificial light has unknowingly become the human organism's secondary synchronizer. It would therefore seem wise to consider the effects of this.

Research Programs Without Light: Underground Environments and Cold Climates

Numerous experiments conducted in caves, isolated rooms, or otherwise dark environments have shown that when deprived of sunlight for a few days, human beings lose all notion of time. In 1962, the speleologist Siffre spent two months in a cave. In his diary, he recounts how he rapidly lost all sense of time: After 40 days, it seemed to him that only 25 days had passed. During a four-month-long experiment conducted in a cave, a woman was active and awake for 20 to 25 hours and asleep for 10 hours, establishing a 30- to 35-hour rest-activity cycle.[31] It would be possible to cite many other experiments of this type, all giving the same results: Although some physiological conditions are capable of maintaining a circadian-type rhythm for a certain length of time, the lack of synchronizers causes human beings to become disoriented. (In the same way, the absence of gravity—i.e., the main spatial references of "above" and "below"—encountered during journeys in outer space causes the human organism to lose its sense of direction. Often, hallucinations are experienced as well, because of the incomprehensibility of the information transmitted by the perceptual apparatus to the brain.) After some weeks, the biological rhythms become separated. Certain hormones continue to be released according to a 25-hour cycle, while the sleep-wake cycle may be interrupted. The activity-rest cycle, normally of a 24-hour duration, may shorten to 16 or lengthen to 30 hours. That is to say, lack of light brings about an internal desynchronization and affects the diencephalic structures that govern on the one hand hormone secretion and on the other the neurotransmitter system.[32] In order to maintain a 24-hour rhythm, the body must be synchronized every day. Light is the most important synchronizer; it is the *zeitgeber,* the marker of time.

In addition to temporal disorientation and the desynchronization of physiological activities, absence of light also causes a depression of tone and mood. This is seen clearly in studies conducted in so-called cold climates, where the constant darkness of the winter months produces mood changes, insomnia, depression, and irregularities in the menstrual cycle. Studies also show that there is a greater frequency of mental illnesses and suicides in populations living at high latitudes. Researchers returning from polar expeditions recount how they personally experienced unusual mood changes, an inability to

Frontispiece. From Athanius Kircher, *Ars magna lucis et umbrae*, Rome, apud Hermannum Scheus, 1646. (Courtesy of Biblioteca Trivulziana, Milan.)

concentrate, and the breakdown of their sleep-wake cycle.[33] Some of these symptoms have now been grouped together and identified as the so-called SAD syndrome (seasonal affective disorder) which is treated by exposure to strong, bright light. According to some researchers, individuals suffering from de-

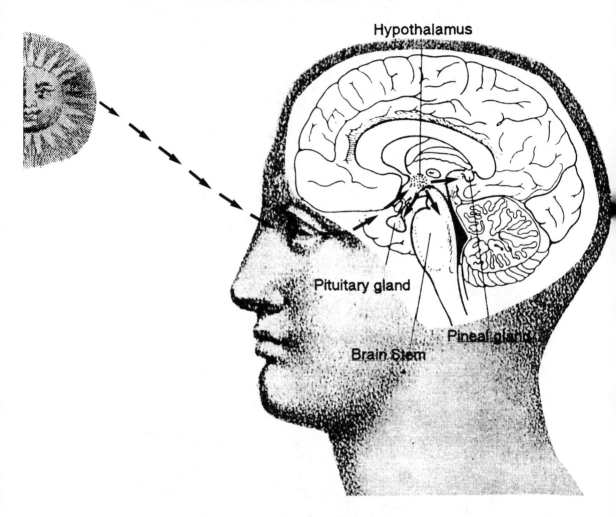

Hypothalamus

Pituitary gland

Pineal gland

Brain Stem

From the sun to the brain.

pression are out of synchrony with circadian rhythms. Treatment therefore consists of attempting to modify their rhythm, influencing their sleep-wake cycle through the use of light.[34]

Exposure for certain periods of time to a light of about 2000 to 2500 lux reduces the secretion of melatonin. It thus corrects temporal imbalance that might have been produced in the body for any number of different reasons (jet lag, night shifts, depression, etc.), producing a sense of well-being. Bright white light has this "stimulatory" power. In his book, *La luce come terapia (Light as Therapy)*, Alessandro Meluzzi cites a study carried out in 1988 in which 12 patients suffering from depression were exposed for a period of one hour on alternate days to either a bright white or weak red light. The results confirmed the therapeutic action of the former.[35] An extract of studies carried out by Meluzzi is reprinted in the appendix. Many doctors are studying the reactions of the human body to light or its absence, with a view to using it therapeutically in the treatment of depression. (Of particular interest in this context are the studies carried out by Czeisler and by Moore, both of Harvard Medical School, and by Brainard, of Jefferson Medical School.)

From the Sun to the Brain, from the Brain to the Body

As light hits the retina, a series of electric impulses transmit this information to the brain and, in particular, the suprachiasmatic nuclei and pineal body. It is thought that the suprachiasmatic nuclei send information by means of electrical/chemical impulses to different parts of the brain (to other

Iconographical Interpretation by Van Gutschoven of the structure of the brain according to Descartes. From René Descartes, *L'homme et un traitté de la formation du foetus [. . .] avec les remarques du louys de la forge [. . .] sur le traitté de l'homme de René Descartes, e sur les figures par luy inventees*, Paris, chez Theodore Girard, 1664. (Courtesy of Biblioteca Universitaria, Bologna.)

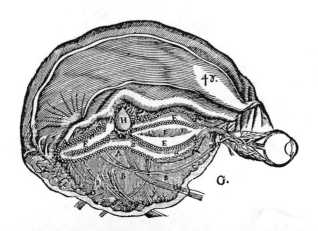

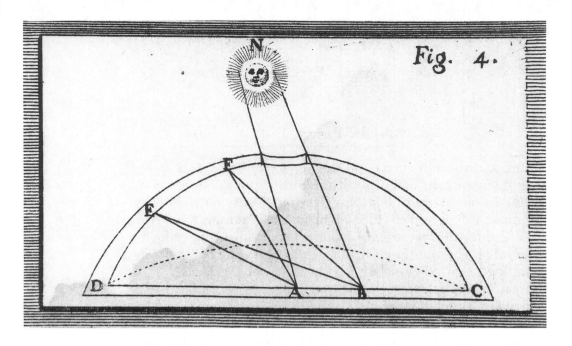

(Above, below and on the following two pages): Studies of the reflections of light. From Leonardo da Vinci, *Trattato della pittura di Leonardo da Vinci nuovamente dato in luce con la vita dello stesso autore scritta da Raffael du Fresne*, Bologna, Istituto delle Scienze, 1786. (Courtesy of Biblioteca Comunale, Milan.)

areas of the hypothalamus, pituitary gland, and pineal body). These areas, in their turn, send hormonal signals to control centers such as the heart, suprarenal glands, liver, kidneys, and intestine. The superchiasmatic nuclei are believed to be the pacemaker responsible for establishing the various rhythms of the body, coordinating them with each other and with the earth's rotation. The pineal body registers the vari-

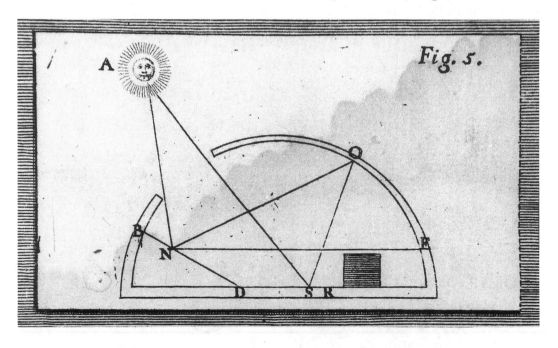

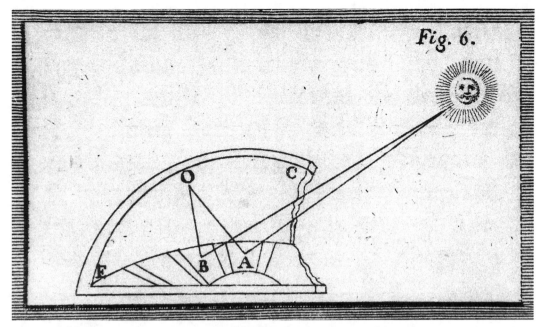

Fig. 6.

ations of light in the environment that are perceived by the retina and transforms the nervous stimuli into hormonal substances, transmitting information about the length and intensity of the light rays. When darkness is perceived, melatonin is produced and similarly, exposure to very bright light causes a rapid drop in its levels.[36]

Secondary Synchronizers

Is it possible, in a confined environment and in the absence of sunlight, to synchronize our biological clock and

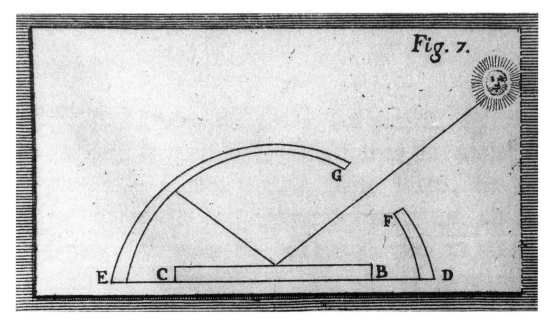

Fig. 7.

maintain our body's rhythmical structure and balance? It would seem that it is. In certain circumstances, it is possible to substitute secondary synchronizers for the primary synchronizer. Experiments on animals have demonstrated that biological rhythms may be modified by environmental factors that operate like secondary synchronizers.[37] In human beings,

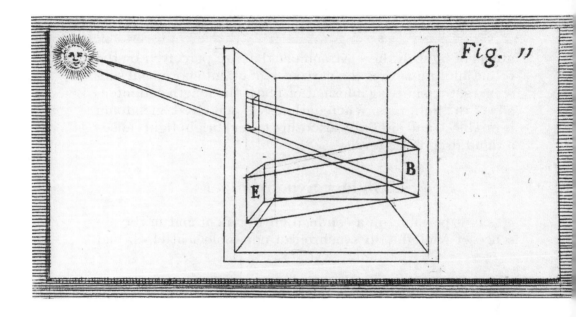

Fig. 11

the synchronization of rhythmical activities is more complex because it is not solely dependent on ecological-environmental factors, but on factors of a social, religious, and cultural nature as well. Not that this diminishes the importance of the so-called secondary synchronizers, however. As the astronaut Poliakov has shown recently,[38] wherein there is no lighting system that reproduces some of the characteristics of sunlight, and no substitute for the earth's spatial-temporal references exists; astronauts are unable to sustain their work capacity and indeed may not even be able to survive in outer space. The same conclusion has been reached by researchers at NASA and ESA engaged in the study of habitability problems encountered during space missions. Secondary synchronizers may be capable of attenuating the problems created by the lack of primary synchronizers.

Contact with Reality

Light does not only permit us to see, it also links the human organism to its surroundings by means of a series of nervous stimuli. It has a direct influence, as we have seen, on a very important gland situated inside the human brain: the pineal gland. Descartes considered this gland to be the meeting point, the linking organ, between the two essences that make up the human being: the *res cogitans* and *res extensa*. We now know from psychoendocrinological studies that the pineal body does indeed function as a link—between the organism and the exterior environment. In technical terms, the pineal gland is a "photosensitive neuroendocrine transducer" whose activity is set in motion by the light-dark cycle. That is to say, it transforms nervous stimuli into a hormonal substance called melatonin. (According to current research, melatonin is concerned with the regulation of the sleep-wake cycle and plays a major role at an immunological level.)[39] The task of the pineal gland and melatonin is in fact to regulate, by means of the perception of light and darkness, biological adaptation to environmental conditions. Another element that functions as a mediator in our relationship with the surrounding environment is color. Indeed, it might be said that this is the task of the senses in general.

Seen "in this light," the job of designing lighting for confined environments is of great importance. However as far as work environments are concerned, the sole preoccupation seems instead to be with ensuring a level of lighting that allows words to be read, letters to be distinguished one from the other, and avoids problems of glare or reflection on VDUs.

Absolutely no consideration is given to the synchronizing function of light, not even in those situations where there are no windows, or in which people are working night shifts.

This brief mention of the psychoendocrinological aspects of the light-organism relationship is important in that it helps us to regard light as something more than simply a means by which to see, and to consider its proper reproduction as a task of greater complexity than is currently supposed.

Lighting in Hospitals

A good deal of research has been carried out demonstrating that exposure to high levels of wide spectrum artificial light may have a beneficial effect on individuals suffering from various illnesses (depression, migraines, jet lags, disrupted sleep patterns, ailments caused by working a night shift, etc.), thanks to the ability of light to act on the endocrine system. Studies in this field are very recent and there has not yet been time for a systematic comparison of the results. Their application is consequently still sporadic. The fact remains, however, that these studies may provide valuable indicators, especially in the planning of special-purpose spaces such as hospitals and convalescence centers.

In his *Human Factors and Lighting,* Peter Boyce cites an interesting experiment carried out by Dr. L.M. Wilson's team in two hospitals in Arkansas. A careful examination was made of 50 patients in two different intensive care wards, one of which had no windows. The age and physical condition of both groups were similar and both were subjected to the same treatment. Wilson found that 40 percent of the patients in the ward without windows developed postoperative fever, as compared to 18 percent of the patients in the ward with windows. In the latter group, the great majority of patients developed simpler forms of postoperative depression. In hospitals where patients spend most of their time in bed, and thus in surroundings in which there is little movement or activity, the absence of windows may give rise to acute environmental dissatisfaction and cause depressed mental states.[40]

Light influences our mood and behavior. And it is a well known fact that a patient's spirit is an important factor in his recovery. It is therefore imperative that, in hospitals especially, consideration be given to problems of a psychological as well as a functional nature (adequate illumination, washable surfaces that allow for easy maintenance and good hygiene). This is extremely important since patients, in their infirm and therefore weak state, are particularly sensitive to environmental conditions. It has to be emphasized that this is not a question of aesthetics. What must be created in a hospital is not a sense of beauty, or at least not only that, but rather an attitude of positive thought and vitality.

How can this be done? One small example: We know all too well that there are some light sources which make our skin look drab and lifeless and throw a leaden, livid light on the surroundings (fluorescent light, e.g., with its cold color tones and low level of illumination). It is not rare to find this type of light being used in hospitals. And yet skin color is one of the reference parameters indicated by the Commission International de l'Eclarage (CIE) for determining the color-rendering index of different light sources (the color-rendering index is a measure of the accuracy with which a color is reproduced by a light source). There are two criteria for the selection of a light source for environments in which the perception of colors is of great importance: Either one chooses a light source with a high color rendering, that is, one that is capable of rendering colors in a way that is very nearly faithful to how they are perceived in natural light; or one deliberately chooses a light source that renders colors in a distorted way, on the basis of the principle that the sky looks nicer if it is very blue (as is the case, e.g., in shops selling food, particularly meat, where the light spectrum of

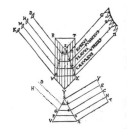

Experiment with the refraction of a light beam as it passes through a prism. From Athanius Kircher, *Ars magna lucis et umbrae*, Rome, apud Hermannum Scheus, 1646. (Courtesy of Biblioteca Trivulziana, Milan.)

the combined sources has to emphasize the red color and filter out any green tones). As far as the latter criteria are concerned, the situation is complicated by the fact that what some researchers have de-fined as a "color discrimination index" does not exist, or at least is not officially recognized, although the importance of such a measuring system is widely acknowledged in the field of lighting design.[41]

This is only one of the aspects to be evaluated in designing the lighting system for an environment. Naturally, a lighting system designed to "put the color back in patients' cheeks" might not be a very attractive proposition, but the point is that artificial light does in fact color. It would therefore seem preferable if people had a lively hue to look at rather than a pale greenish one (which is depressing). And this is only one of the aspects to be considered in designing a lighting system. The elaboration of parameters that could be referred to when designing a new hospital or convalescent center would be an important contribution and invaluable to the architect who is often working on a tight schedule and with a restricted budget, and without any other points of reference other than his or her own aesthetic judgment. Drawing up a system of measurement for everything that concerns the psychological aspects of the perception of light and color is an important task.

The figure represents the sun, scale of wavelength, visible spectrum, and refraction of light through a prism. The visible zone of the spectrum is situated between the infrared and ultraviolet zones (between 780 and 380 nanometers). The visible spectrum can be roughly divided into a series of wavelength intervals that correspond to different sensations of color: 380 to 440 nanometers = purple; 440 to 500 nanometers = blue; 500 to 570 nanometers = green; 570 to 590 nanometers = yellow; 590 to 630 nanometers = orange; and 630 to 780 nanometers = red. The unit of measurement is hertzian waves and the nanometer (nm) [1 nanometer = 10]. From Manuale di illuminotecnica I Guzzini, Ancona, Sagraf, 1987. (Courtesy of I Guzzini Illuminazione.)

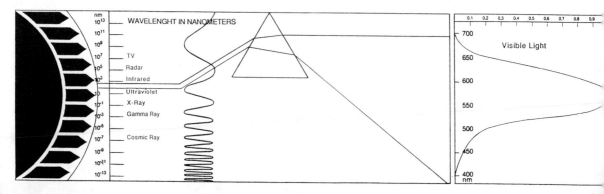

The Perception of Light and Color

Light forms a small part of the electromagnetic energy travelling through space. It is registered within the electromagnetic spectrum between radio waves (which have longer wavelengths) and X-rays (which have shorter wavelengths). To be precise, light is a portion of electromagnetic energy produced by cosmic rays, with a wavelength measuring between 360 and 780 nanometers. An electromagnetic wave is a small quantity of energy travelling through space. A two-dimensional illustration of the way in which it moves may be seen in the concentric waves produced when a stone is thrown into still water. The energy and frequency of visible electromagnetic wavelengths are visualized and registered by the spectrum. What is special about these wavelengths is that they are intercepted by the human visual apparatus, producing the phenomenon of vision. In speaking of light and color, we are basically referring to human perception, for although the phenomenon of light is also studied in physics, only a part of the problem—and the least complex part at that—is examined.

Color

Is color a feeling? Color is something that is perceived by the human visual apparatus when it encounters certain wavelengths of electromagnetic energy. Color is the result of a very special relationship between the electromagnetic spectrum and human perceptual apparatus. In fact, it is a mistake to speak of color in relation to animals, despite the fact that some species of animals display beautiful colors. Humans perceive the various hues of the scales of certain fish as colors, but we do not know how fish perceive them. Color is the result of the very special and unique way in which human vision perceives the electromagnetic spectrum between 360 and 780 nanometers. How this happens is determined by the conformation of and the characteristics inherent in the visual apparatus of the human brain. The eyes and brains of fish and insects have very different characteristics. Although it is true that they perceive electromagnetic waves, it is mistaken to say that they perceive color.

Relation to the Theory of Music

> Colour and sound . . . are like two rivers which have their source in one and the same mountain, but subsequently pursue their way under totally different conditions in two totally different regions, so that throughout the whole course of both no two points can be compared.[42]

From the point of view of physics, there are a number of similarities between sound waves and light waves. For example, they travel in the same way, albeit at a different wavelength and by different means (unlike light, sound does not travel in a vacuum). The most important differences concern if anything the way in which they are received by the human perceptual apparatus. For example, by pressing together all the keys of a piano, we produce sounds that we can perceive as being different, one from the other (high notes, low notes, etc.). In the same way, we are able to say whether one key or 10 are being pressed. It is not the same with light. The same blue-green color may be produced, without our being aware of it, by single wavelengths with different characteristics as well as by several wavelengths. Human beings have the ability to analyze the sound spectrum with a high degree of precision, but they are unable to do likewise with the light spectrum.

Science and Color Perception

In order to put light and color perception in a scientific perspective, we must first gain an exact understanding of the physiological bases of our sensory perceptions. Take the sense of taste for example. We know quite well what the difference in taste is between a strawberry and an apple or between a carrot and a potato, but not in a scientific way. We have not yet sufficient knowledge for understanding the physiological basis of this process. Much research has been done by space agencies to place the senses—taste, smell, color, perception, etc.—within a scientific framework. But so far, rather than provide concrete results, research of this type has simply opened doors and indicated further sectors for study.

Given the impossibility of analyzing the human perceptual system through a microscope, the best we can do is study it indirectly. In order to understand how human beings perceive color, researchers in color science (which is the study of how to reproduce colors and is based on what is known about light and color, from both a physical and perceptual point of view) conduct experiments that basically consist of asking individuals to match colors. The point of color science tests is not to discover a person's favorite color. It is simply to find out how an individual perceives two different spectra. It seems a simple problem, but actually much remains to be discovered about this process: In fact, it can happen that spectra with different characteristics are perceived as one and the same color.

Conducting experiments on the way in which people match or distinguish colors seems trivial in comparison with a problem as complex and fascinating as the perception of color. However, already the limited knowledge gained in this field has allowed the automobile, photography, advertising, and computer industries to conceive and sell advanced-technology products that play a fundamental role in the environments in which we live and work. An understanding of color science is, for example, of prime importance in the automobile industry. Insignificant though it may seem, the purchase and therefore the choice of an automobile are also determined by the fact that the color of the exterior is a perfect match with the color of the interior. The color of the dashboard, door handle, seat and carpet, gearstick, etc.—all the elements that make up the inside of an automobile—must match in order to produce an overall uniformity of color, regardless of the fact that each element is constructed of a different material and manufactured by a different company, often in different locations. The producer of automobile components has to know how to achieve matching colors. And to succeed in this, he has to understand the connection or relationship between light and color, and between the electromagnetic spectrum and perceptual apparatus; in other words, he has to have an understanding of the laws of color science.

The same is true for companies operating in the field of photography or technological image reproduction (which are

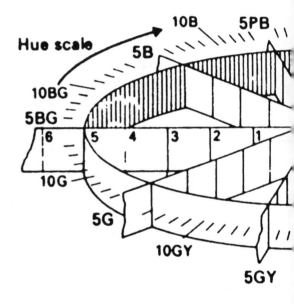

(*Above and facing page*): This is the method that allows identification with the greatest precision (currently possible) of a given color. In this way, instead of saying, for example, that you want a yellow-green material, it is possible to refer to the Munsell color scale: 5YG/8/2. The hue letters are PB = purple/blue, p = purple, RP = red/purple, R = red, YR = yellow/red, GY = green/yellow, G = green, and BG = blue/green. (Courtesy of Peter Boyce.)

both methods of reproducing the phenomenon of vision) as well as computers. Researchers in computer science are currently looking for a way to reproduce "accurate colors," that is, colors that are similar to real colors. At present, colors are

Value scale

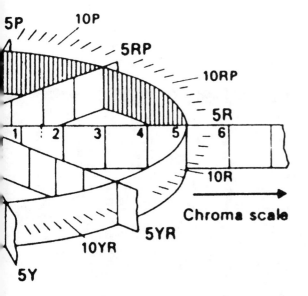

5P

10P

5RP

10RP

5R

1 2 3 4 5 6

10R

Chroma scale

5YR

10YR

5Y

described as portions of red, green, and blue energy combined with each other, and it is not yet possible to identify them precisely. Color science is used also in the field of advertising. An interesting study in this regard has been conducted in Japan. A person was fitted with an instrument that, by means of a microtelecamera, could follow the movements of the pupils. The aim of the experiment was to discover which products were the first to attract the shopper's attention in a supermarket. The extraordinary device revealed that the pupils were immediately, almost physiologically attracted by the colors of boxes of detergent. We are indeed more sensitive to some colors than others. Research has confirmed that advertisers have a very good grasp of color science.

The term "easy eye green" has become something of a byword in the United States as far as the perception of colors is concerned. It was the basis on which hospitals substituted the white color of their walls and uniforms for green, with the aim of minimizing the after-image effects reported by operating theatre staff. According to the results of an in-depth study of the perception of light and color carried out by Jim

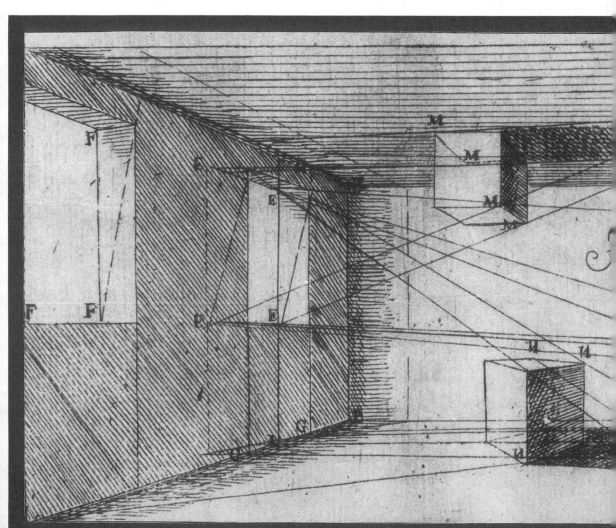

Wise, a NASA researcher working on the problems of space habitability, it is not so much the color hue (i.e., the color green) that is important in operating theatres, but its degree of lightness. Another color with the same degree of lightness might produce the same if not better results.[43]

Numerous experiments have been conducted that confirm the relaxing effect of the color green. Among these, one of the most interesting was the experiment carried out by Robert Gerard.[44] A group of 24 men was asked to look at a screen on

(*Below and facing page*): Study by Ferdinando Galli Bibiena on the effects of natural and artificial light, incident rays, and shadows. From Ferdinando Galli Bibiena, *L'architettura civile preparata su la geometria e ridotta alla prospettiva*, Parma, Paolo Monti, 1711. (Courtesy of Biblioteca Trivulziana, Milan.)

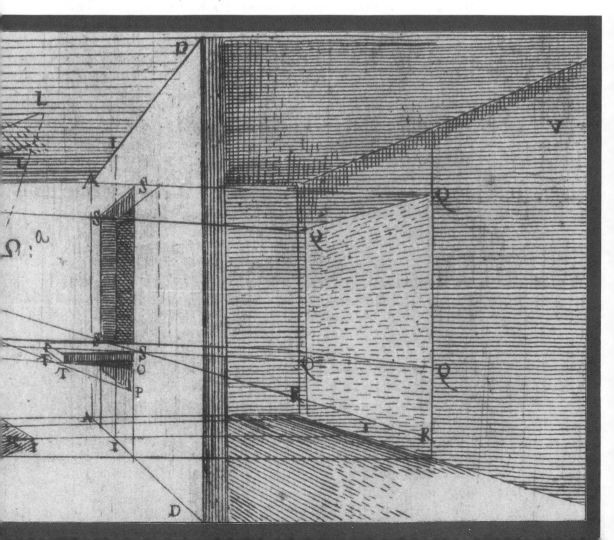

which was projected a series of red, blue, and white lights in turn. The men had to look at each light for 10 minutes while the following physiological data were recorded: blood pressure, respiration rate, heartbeat, blink frequency, and an electro-encephalogram. Gerard found that, with the exception of the heartbeat, the physiological conditions varied from the red condition to the blue condition. Blood pressure went down when the subjects perceived the blue light, and at the same time their respiration and blink rate dropped, while alpha waves increased. The red light stimulated a more alert state of mind, the blue light a more relaxed one. On the basis of these experiments, Gerard gave further confirmation of the sedative effect of blue light on a psycho-physiological level (although we do not know what type of light he used, or what he intended by the "color blue"). In his famous book on color, Itten cites experiments conducted with human beings as well as animals that give further confirmation of the physiological effect produced by certain colors, and in particular by red and blue.[45]

Researchers in several American universities are currently working on the perception of light and color. At the University of Arkansas, Nancy Kwallek's team is collaborating on a research project with NASA to determine the colors to be used in the interior of the space station Freedom. Kwallek's experiments, which have only recently got underway, are based on the assumption that "value" (the quantity of white and black) and "saturation" (color intensity) are the characteristics that exert the most influence on the human perception of color. Not only certain colors, therefore, or certain juxtapositions of color, but also (let us say) certain degrees of color may have a positive or negative influence on our productivity. Other studies are examining the role played by color and light at a cognitive level (sense of direction, mental lucidity) and psychological level (claustrophobia, anxiety).[46]

Color can also influence the perception of time. The French Impressionists were the first to discover this possibility, creating, by means of the juxtaposition of complementary colors, a sense of the present. The placing of two complementary colors side by side—colors that are at opposite ends of the spectrum from each other—has the effect of stimulating the eye, and therefore also the perceptive mind, to its most active state (a fact that seems, as we have seen, to have been thoroughly mastered by those responsible for the packaging of detergents). Studies of the perception of light and color have also been made by environmental psychologists. A number of experiments have been conducted into the influence that light and color may exert on sense of direction, mood, and behavior.[47] Even now, much work is being done in order to verify the effects of color on productivity. The rich bibliography compiled by Wise on color research conducted for NASA is witness to the great number of studies in this field.

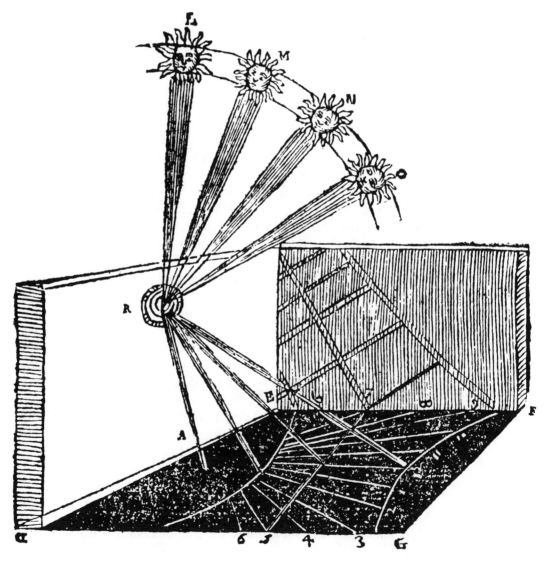

Sundial. From Athanius Kircher, *Ars magna lucis et umbrae*, Rome, apud Hermannum Scheus, 1646. (Courtesy of Biblioteca Trivulziana, Milan.)

Environments and Colors

As we have said, some of the most technologically advanced products on the market are the result of the application
of the laws of color science. There is one field, however, that
seems completely to ignore these laws: architectural design.
Color science is used in the production of objects but not the
definition of spaces. And yet the space and lightness of an
environment are not independent from its colors and surfaces.
Lighting has to be understood as meaning something more
complex than simply the total sum of light sources. Often, the
word "lighting" is used to mean the luminous quality of an
environment. In fact, the light spectrum that our eye perceives
is the product of the intermingling of light spectra coming from
both direct light sources as well as surfaces in the environment.
What we perceive as a room's luminosity is therefore the result
of a process that involves light, colors, and surfaces.

Interesting in this context is the modification carried out
on an ice hockey stadium where the lighting had the sole aim
of allowing the players to see the puck. The problem was that
the spectators could not visually differentiate the environment
as a whole, since the ice, walls, and ceiling were of the same
brightness and the same color. In order to alleviate the spectators' discomfort, it was decided to paint the reticulated
beams holding up the roof of the stadium red. The problem
was not strictly one of lighting, but concerned rather the visual
environment. Lighting is only one of the many factors in its
creation. Light can play a vital role in creating a feeling and is
a positive experience only when it is seen as a component part
of an environment. This is why Boyce writes of "the illusion of
luminance": to point to the impossibility of creating an environment that is satisfying from the point of view of lighting
simply by following lighting design standards.

In his Color Theory, Goethe writes:

> People experience a great delight in colour, generally. The
> eye requires it as much as it requires light. We have only to
> remember the refreshing sensation we experience, if on a
> cloudy day the sun illumines a single portion of the scene

before us and displays its colours. That healing powers were ascribed to coloured gems, may have arisen from the experience of this indefinable pleasure. . . . Experience teaches us that particular colours excite particular states of feeling. In order to experience these influences completely, the eye should be entirely surrounded with one colour; we should be in a room of one colour, or look through a coloured glass. We are then identified with the hue, it attunes the eye and mind in mere unison with itself. The colours on the *plus* side are yellow, red, orange. . . . The feelings they excite are quick, lively, aspiring. . . . In its highest purity (yellow) always carries with it the nature of brightness, and has a serene, gay, softly exciting character. . . . The red-yellow gives an impression of warmth and gladness. . . . In looking steadfastly at a perfect yellow-red surface, the colour seems actually to penetrate the organ. It produces an extreme excitement. . . . Rooms which are hung with pure blue, appear in some degree larger, but at the same time empty and cold. . . . This unquiet feeling increases as the hue progresses, and it may be safely assumed that a carpet of a perfectly pure deep blue-red would be intolerable. . . . (Red) conveys an impression of gravity and dignity, and at the same time of grace and attractiveness. . . . Surrounding accompaniments of this colour have always a grave and magnificent effect. . . . The eye and the mind repose (on green). Hence for rooms to live in constantly, the green colour is most generally selected.[48]

Color gives pleasure, it can excite and depress, it can stimulate or produce states of calm or unease. Finally, color can facilitate our relationship with reality and the surrounding environment. Much of what Goethe wrote about in the eighteenth century is familiar to us through personal experience. However, data concerning the perception of light and color from a psychological-cognitive point of view still lack any kind of systematic organization, not to mention a scientific framework.

As early as 1981, in his *Human Factors in Lighting,* Boyce complained about the lack of a color discrimination and color preference index. Boyce stressed the importance of arriving at additional measurement systems for light, based on the theories being advanced by researchers in the field. He also noted that the index of color rendering had after all, like other measurement techniques officially accepted by the CIE, begun life as an idea.[49] In much the same way as researchers are working toward a definition of accurate colors in the various industrial sectors, architects too could attempt to transfer, or translate into planning instruments, the knowledge gained so far in the field of color science. The point may even be reached in which it becomes possible to give precise indications as to the lighting and colors to be used in a given space, whether internal or external: the intensity and type of light sources, advice about which colors might be used in order to stimulate not only certain sensations, but moods, behavior, and improved physical performance as well. This could be an opportunity to dispel the prejudice that the architect's task is solely aesthetic, and to show convincingly that good architecture, properly planned interiors, and well-conceived lighting constitute a social service of considerable importance. The terms "good," "proper," and "well-conceived" as used here apply to the construction of buildings and environments that promote the psychological and physiological well-being of people.

(*Right and facing page*): Trompe l'oeil, Tunnel Discotheque, New York City, 1986. (Photo: Dida Biggi.)

CHAPTER 5

DESIGN OF WINDOWLESS ENVIRONMENTS

There are some environments in our cities in which the total lack of natural light is not a problem, for example, discos. Here, the lack of sensory stimuli produced by sunlight is compensated for by special effects created by artificial light and music. Another environment that is purposely lacking in nat-

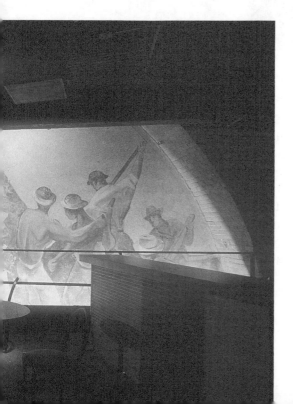

(*Above left and above*): Windows are all-important elements in spatial perception, for both light and the perspective depth they offer, capable of making even a small space seem larger. Office of Sandro Marpillero, New York City, 1992. (Photo: Sandro Marpillero.)

ural light is the cinema or theatre. Here, the absence of windows permits a better view and also helps people to enter into the unreal and magical dimension created by the action on stage or screen. Essentially, these are places of entertainment and one's sojourn inside them is limited to a few hours. There are other types of environments, however, in which the completely artificial nature of the lighting constitutes a problem. There are two ways of approaching the problem of lighting a windowless environment. One way is to use devices that conduct sunlight into them, and another is to try to compensate for the lack of natural light by using artificial light in a particular way. Some contemporary architects have experimented with various ways of bringing the sun's rays inside their buildings: For example, Norman Foster created a series of "sun traps" for the Hong Kong Shanghai Bank that collect sunlight and deflect it, by means of a system of mirrors or reflecting surfaces, into the building's interior. The offices of the Underground Space Center at the University of Minnesota boast an atrium that, despite being situated 30 meters underground, is lit by natural light thanks to a special refraction system. Another way of admitting sunlight into a windowless environment is by means of optic fibers (which are linked to a series of lenses outside the building and a solar tracker that follows the course of the sun so that the lenses are hit directly by its rays). Optic fibers are currently at the center of much research. The second approach, that of compensating for the lack of natural light by wholly artificial means, is more complex.

THE SIVRA LABORATORY

The SIVRA Laboratory is a lighting design laboratory built in Recanati, Italy in 1991 dedicated exclusively to the development of lighting systems for use in windowless environments. It is specially equipped to conduct experiments and take measurements on the color variation (color temperature) and intensity (level of illumination) of light. The aim is to impart to artificial lighting systems those qualities of variability and changeability that are to be found in natural light.[50]

Artificial light conditions our way of perceiving space. In windowless environments, the planning of lighting systems

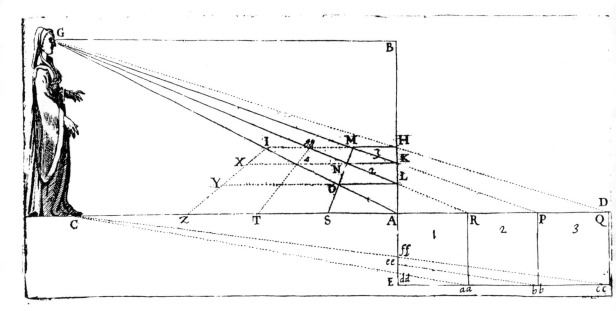

(*Above and facing page*): Perspective-based drawing. From Jacopo Barozzi (Vignola), *Le due regole della prospettiva pratica coi commenti di I. Danti,* Rome, Mascardi Printing House, 1644. (Courtesy of Biblioteca Comunale, Milan.)

naturally cannot be restricted simply to the choice of light sources, the positioning of lights, or defining parameters for lighting design. When there is no natural light, there are no windows; thus, a fundamental architectural element is missing. Windows allow us to perceive a deep space, stretching beyond the room, beyond the building itself. To substitute for the window, it is not enough to paint in a fake one (although this technique has also been tried). Instead, the spatial and lighting characteristics of a window have to be reproduced, using the terms of reference supplied by research conducted in confined environments: using, we might say, "secondary synchronizers and spatial references." The presence of a window means the possibility of having natural light inside an environment, seeing the panorama outside, having fresh air, feeling in touch with the outside world. And, at another level, this means mental stimulation, not feeling isolated. All these are not simply superfluous pleasure that one can do without; rather, they are "stimuli information" of fundamental importance for the equilibrium of the organism. Planning the lighting of a windowless environment is a task that must be undertaken along with detailed planning of the space.

Normally, the laboratories used for experimenting with light are of a totally uniform white or gray color. The shape of the SIVRA Laboratory instead shows certain variations that should be employed in the planning of windowless environments. In the absence of natural light, what is required above all else are wide spaces and high ceilings, in order to counter feelings of claustrophobia. In a small, enclosed space, representations may be used (affording the same type of pleasure as the photograph of a loved one in his or her absence gives). In order to give the illusion of more space, one wall was decorated with a large tromp l'oeil painting, interchangeable with a sim-

Floorplan, SIVRA Laboratory, I Guzzini Illuminazione, Recanati, Italy, 1992. Architects: Piera Scuri, Douglas Skene, and Daniele Bedini. Drawing by Douglas Skene.

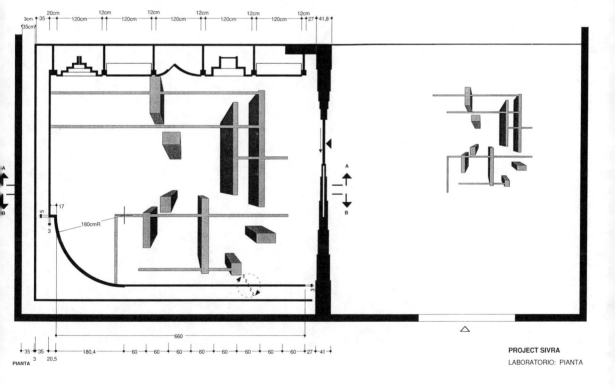

ilarly sized geometric perspective design, this time realized in
ceramic tiles. The ceiling and walls of the hall have an irregular surface made up of a series of oblique panels painted in

Interior view, SIVRA Laboratory I Guzzini Illuminazione, Recanati, Italy, 1992. Architects: Piera Scuri, Douglas Skene, and Daniele Bedini. (Photo: Douglas Skene.)

different tonalities of gray. Instead of being emitted by lamps or other objects, light comes from a series of horizontal and vertical openings in the ceiling and walls. One wall is covered in differently colored panels ranging from cold tones on one side to warm tones on the other. These are used to study the effect of different combinations of light sources on different colors. The light spectrum perceived by our eyes is not produced solely by the light source, but by the combination of direct light and light reflected off the walls. The colors and surfaces of an environment are therefore very important. As stated previously, the absence of stimuli produced by natural light and windows has to be compensated for by a series of contrivances introduced in the planning stages. These contrivances affect both small details as well as the more important elements of the environment. The very texture of the materials making up our surroundings is important for

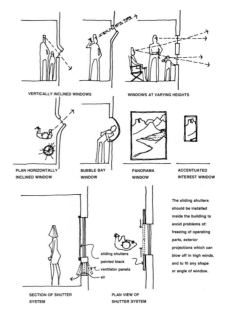

stimulating our senses. For this reason, inside the SIVRA Laboratory, the surfaces of walls and furnishings have been treated in such a way as to give them a "peach skin" texture that is slightly soft to the touch.

The aim of the research conducted at the SIVRA Laboratory, it has to be emphasized, is not to initiate a mass building program of windowless structures, but to create more advanced lighting systems, starting from the premise that natural light plays a very much richer and more complex role than simply that of illuminating space.

(*Above right*): Windows, sketches. From Leon Zrudio, *Psychological Problems and Environmental Design in the North*, Université Laval, Quebec, Canada. (Courtesy of Leon Zrudio.)

DESIGN OF WINDOWLESS
CONTROL ROOMS

Control room, Enichem Elastomeri, Ferrara, Italy, 1990. Architects: Piera Scuri and Douglas Skene.

The control rooms of industrial plants are particularly interesting in that they evince aspects of contemporary work environments that would otherwise be invisible. Control rooms are often isolated from the surrounding environment and the plant itself by thick cement walls and reinforced doors. But all offices and work environments in which the windows are sealed and light and air produced artificially the whole year round are also, to a certain extent, isolated. Most of the activity that goes on in a control room involves interaction with advanced technologies. In the same way, work environments in which activity centers mainly around computers are becoming more and more common. In control rooms, certain basic problems inherent in the environments in which we live and work are magnified in such a way as to become very apparent. In the same way, every abnormal condition makes the comprehension of normal conditions possible.

Man–Machine System

Work environments in which people interact with advanced technologies are particularly stressful for the human body. In fact, in a purely virtual dimension such as that of the control room operator, it seems as if only the head is at work, while the body and space are often neglected. What happens as a result is that, for the sake of efficiency and economy, the rooms and corridors end up being rectangular in shape, with raised floors, lowered ceilings, and walls constructed exclusively of plastic materials. Absolutely no consideration is given to the nature of the space. Only rarely do architects ever enter industrial complexes: The on-site offices and other work environments are often little more than sheds.

As a result, environments are created that are simple to plan, easy to put up and take down, and very economical, but which hinder productivity and destroy creativity. And yet interest in so-called human resources and plant safety makes the study of space and the environmental characteristics necessary for total work efficiency obligatory. The control room does not end at the edge of the operator's chair. Indeed, there are few places in which space appears so disintegrated and broken up as in industrial plants, perhaps because industrial plants represent the triumph of "process" over "form." Industrial plants are like overgrown stills that have blown up the laboratory, the building, the area of town, and have rooted themselves in the earth, invading the streets with their tubes and ducts and valves and cylinders. All around them, clutching their helmets and work tools, scurry frightened little human beings.

Without Windows

One of the fundamental problems for operators in windowless control rooms is not having a direct view of the complex, this having disappeared along with the large glass panel that characterized the former type of control room. Of course, within the control room there are a number of representations of the plant (computerized images, plant status boards, and TV monitors wired to telecameras focused on the plant). However, as far as the operator is concerned, the sight of a valve opening is one thing, whereas it is quite another to see this operation represented by a flashing light. A danger that is seen, felt, and smelled produces reactions of a very different sort from one that is signalled by the intermittent flashing of a lightbulb. This is especially true if it happens for instance in a moment in which the operator is drowsy, perhaps on account of the late hour or because he has spent the whole night under the constant glare of row upon row of overhead fluorescent lights. The representations used may not be enough to provoke the type of reaction needed, especially in emergency situations. It is therefore of vital importance to create an environment that keeps the operator in a state of reality, in other words, in an environment that is sensorially stimulating. Smells, sounds, tactile sensations, vistas, variety, changes in light, etc. are all stimuli that maintain cerebral activity and are absent in a confined environment.

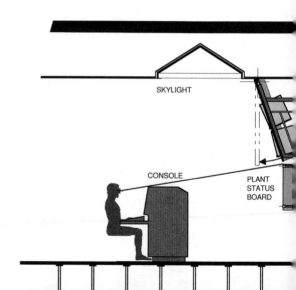

The Human Factor

It is a fact, as the numerous studies carried out by the Electric Power Research Institute (EPRI) in America have

Detail. (Photo: Dida Biggi.)

established, that consideration of human factors in the planning of control rooms for industrial, electric, or nuclear plants means lessening the probability of human error and improving plant safety. The Three Mile Island accident, documented in the Kemeny Commission report, drew attention to problems of human origin in nuclear and industrial plants. In the wake of the accident, special regulations were drawn up in the United States for the design of control rooms, while the EPRI published a human engineering guide that attempted to integrate principles related to human factors with the normal planning criteria for nuclear plants. The idea of this guide is to allow planners to make use of empirically based knowledge about human interaction with advanced technology, with the ultimate aim of maximizing the efficiency of the system, both in normal and emergency situations.[51] Another outcome of Three Mile Island was that in France, a team of experts was entrusted with the task of investigating the causes of accidents in nuclear power plants. The results of their analysis formed the basis for a series of planning recommendations that have proved extremely useful: In the past few years, the number of accidents in French nuclear plants has been significantly reduced. All this goes to show how consideration of the so-called human factor is of the greatest importance in planning environments in which human beings interact with advanced technologies that perform control functions.

Reality/Representation: Virtual Reality

The role of the control room is central to the operations of an industrial complex. Enclosed within four walls of rein-

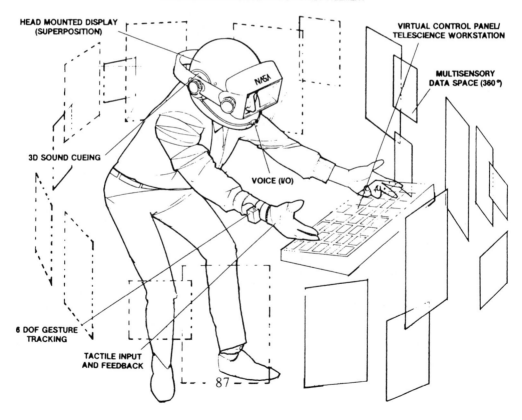

Visual interface environment. (Courtesy of NASA.)

forced concrete, it stands on the outer limits of the complex and is linked to the latter by an enormous number of underground wires, cables, and ducts. The control room is, in a certain sense, a space outside reality, and yet it maintains a vital link with reality (i.e., the reality of the industrial plant), in that it regulates its working. The operator acts upon reality (the plant) by means of a representative medium (e.g., a diagram provided by the computer). Problems may therefore arise if such representations are not sufficient to elicit an opportune reaction in the operator—especially so in emergency situations.

The problems of the man–machine system discussed above with regard to space flights may be seen to arise in this context also, albeit in a more attenuated form. The tasks carried out by control room operators are of a certain difficulty and importance: It is they who are responsible for maintaining control of the plant even in the case of an emergency (when a breakdown occurs). Consequently, they must be able to work, and work efficiently, in potentially dangerous and therefore highly stressful situations. Those operating the control panel must therefore maintain rapid reactions and mental lucidity, despite the fact that the environment in which they work often deprives them of the necessary mental and sensorial stimuli. Actually, it is extremely important to create a series of stimuli in control rooms in order to maintain the operator in a state of reality. It is not simply a problem of interfacing man with machine, or an appropriately designed control panel. These elements are part of the immediate surroundings. The control panel operator turns his head toward the door, gets up to go to the toilet or the desk for a document, goes to eat in the cafeteria, looks at his watch, listens to noises, chats with his colleagues, consults diagrams of the plant, answers the telephone, etc. The operator is bound anyway to perceive the space around him, to be immersed in a particular environment, and to be influenced by it. Being an organism, he is endowed with a number of sensory analyzers that receive stimuli (tactile, auditory, olfactory, mental, etc.) continually from the surrounding environment.

Control room, Enichem Elastomeri, Ferrara, Italy, 1990. Architects: Piera Scuri and Douglas Skene.

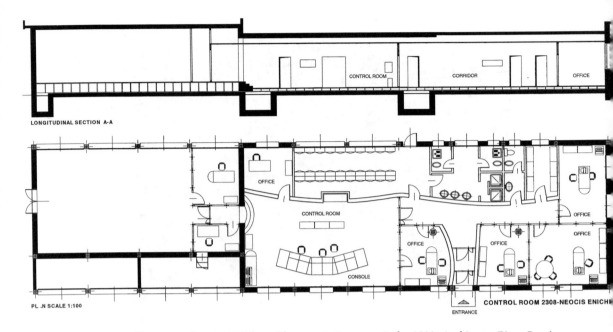

LONGITUDINAL SECTION A-A

OFFICE

CONTROL ROOM

CONTROL ROOM

CONSOLE

CORRIDOR

OFFICE

OFFICE

OFFICE

OFFICE

OFFICE

PL .N SCALE 1:100

ENTRANCE

CONTROL ROOM 2308-NEOCIS ENICHI

Plan, control room, Enichem Elastomeri, Ravenna, Italy, 1992. Architects: Piera Scuri and Douglas Skene.

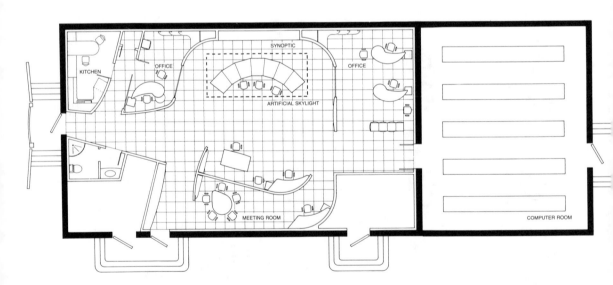

KITCHEN

OFFICE

SYNOPTIC

OFFICE

ARTIFICIAL SKYLIGHT

COMPUTER ROOM

MEETING ROOM

Plan, control room, Himont Italia, Ferrara, Italy, 1989. Architects: Piera Scuri and Douglas Skene.

(*Facing page, top*): Enichem Elastomeri Chemical Plant, Ravenna, Italy. (Courtesy of Papetti.)

(*Facing page, bottom*): Plan, control room, Enichem Elastomeri, Ferrara, Italy, 1990. Architects: Piera Scuri and Douglas Skene.

146

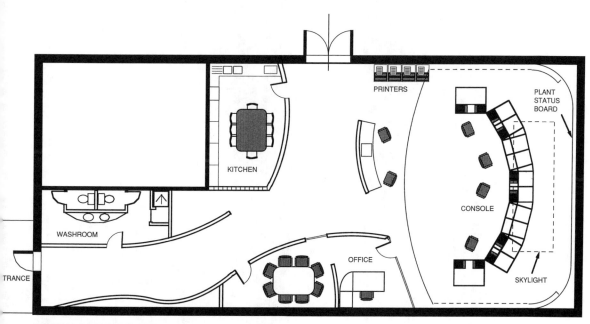

CONTROL ROOM ENICHEM FERRARA
Scale 1:100

High-Technology Work Environments

So how is it possible, within a enclosed environment, to recreate stimuli that more closely resemble those produced by the natural world? Regarding the control room, some studies suggest reproducing within it the noises, even the vibrations,

of the plant's machinery. But there are other ways as well. Certain design features can render highly technological environments less tiring both physically and mentally. The spatial

(*Below and facing page*): Control room, Enichem Elastomeri, Ravenna, Italy, 1992. Architects: Piera Scuri and Douglas Skene.

configuration, lighting, colors, and furnishings may all be used in such a way so as to create a series of stimuli that counter the immobility of the environment. For example, what is the sense in building a brick, wood, or stone wall that is perhaps obliquely set and of varying widths, rather than assembling a series of white or gray plastic partitions that are easy to take down again and maybe even washable? No, it is not just that the former looks nicer, or at least, not only that: It is because it is more stimulating. Good architecture creates powerful sensory as well as mental stimuli. This, after all, is also a characteristic of natural environments (excluding deserts and polar regions), in response to which the human organism has adapted in the course of the centuries. Natural space is a powerful source of sensory and mental stimulation for human beings. Artificial space has to become the same. How? By technological means, obviously, and of the most advanced type. And by utilizing knowledge—from the medical and other fields—about the human organism and the possibilities of creating stimuli with colors, forms, and spatial dimensions. Although it is obviously impossible artificially to recreate nature's variety and continual mutability, it is possible, however, to imitate her better.

Himont Italia and Enichem Elastomeri Control Rooms

The Himont Italia and Enichem Elastomeri industrial plants at Ferrara and Ravenna are regulated by a number of control rooms enclosed in rectangular boxes of reinforced concrete. For safety reasons (resistance to possible explosions), the outside walls have no openings, so the interiors are lit entirely by artificial light. It is imperative that the operators remain constantly alert and maintain rapid reflexes, despite working in an environment characterized by a very low level of sensory stimuli and devoid of temporal rhythm. The preexistent layout of a central corridor with small rectangular rooms on either side made the space seem even smaller and accentuated its principal feature: confinement. Such a spatial configuration increased the sense of suffocation created by a space without openings onto the outside. The ill-chosen furniture, drab colors, and inadequate lighting combined to make the environment even more unpleasant. Following continual complaints from the staff, the Himont and Enichem management asked us to design an environment that responded positively to the needs of its operators. Before embarking on the design phase, various on-the-spot inspections were made, both during the day and night, of the control room interior. On completion of the first stages of the new design, a number of further post-occupancy evaluations allowed us to identify errors and improve on subsequent designs.

Design   With the introduction of a brick wall, the austere concrete boxes were endowed with a series of projections, curves, and apertures. The aim of all the various modifications was basically the same: to counteract the sense of immobility in the environment and increase the number of stimuli. This was achieved above all else by the creation of an asymmetrical layout, allowing the operators to perceive their surroundings in ways that were constantly varied and unexpected. The effect was heightened by the installation of large, explosion-proof glass panels, openings in the walls, and a special lighting system. In the case of the control room at Enichem Elastomeri, particular attention was paid to surface textures (smooth, rough, shiny, opaque) and colors (light gray, dark gray, blue, green, light blue, brown, pink, etc.). In our first control room designs, the need to counter the sense of suffocation caused by isolation had determined the choice of a uniform white color and smooth white surfaces, so as to create a sense of lightness. In the course of post-occupancy evaluations carried out after the plant had gone into production and the control rooms were operating, it was found that, together with a sense of spaciousness, a greater degree of sensory stimulation had also to be created (a fact that was made apparent by the constant presence of transistor radios brought in to work almost furtively by the operators, not as a means of distraction, but as an extreme attempt at providing themselves with some stimulus). Subsequent designs consequently placed more emphasis on surfaces, colors, and materials.

Lighting   As stated earlier, lighting means something more complex than simply the sum total of light sources. The

(*Facing page, top*): Lighting plan, control room, Enichem Elastomeri, Ferrara, Italy, 1990. Architects: Piera Scuri and Douglas Skene.

(*Below, and facing page, bottom*): The effects of light and shade. From Ferdinando Galli Bibbiena, *L'architettura civile preparata sulla geometria e ridotta alla prospettiva*, Parma, Paolo Monti, 1711. (Courtesy of Biblioteca Comunale, Milan.)

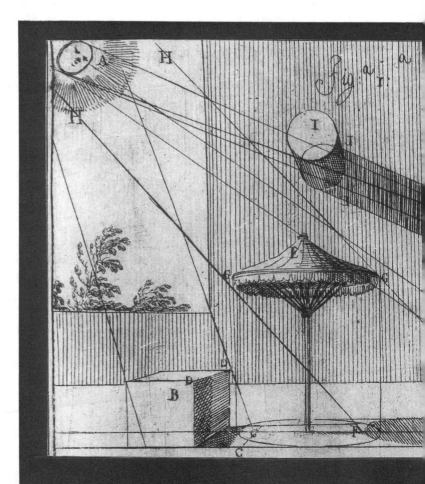

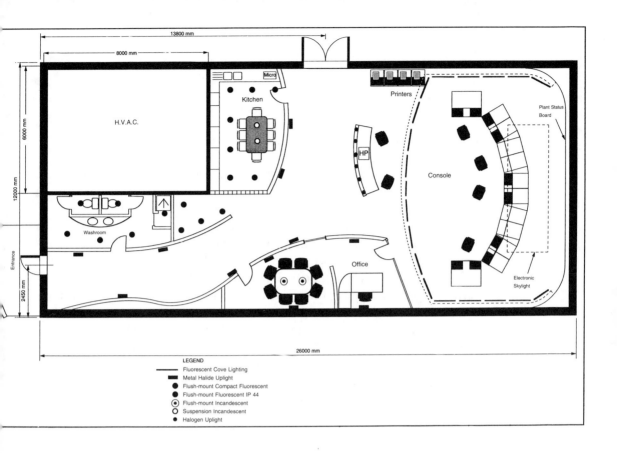

LEGEND
— Fluorescent Cove Lighting
▬ Metal Halide Uplight
● Flush-mount Compact Fluorescent
● Flush-mount Fluorescent IP 44
⊙ Flush-mount Incandescent
○ Suspension Incandescent
● Halogen Uplight

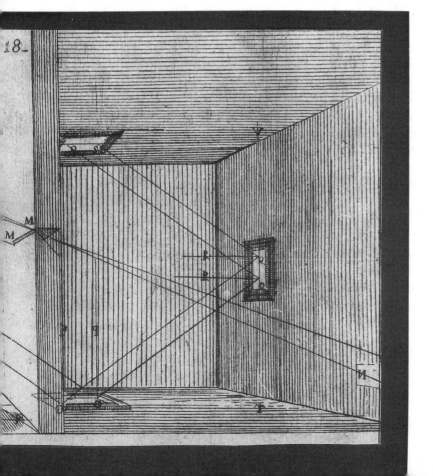

153

term lighting is frequently used to mean the luminous quality of an environment. Indeed, the light spectrum perceived by our eyes is the product of the combination of light spectra from both light sources and surfaces in the environment. Thus, the perception of luminosity in a room is the result of a process in which light, colors, and surfaces are all involved.

In a windowless control room, the lighting system assumes special importance. And not only because of the need to avoid such nuisances as reflection on computer screens: An attempt must also be made to reproduce some of the characteristics of natural light that are important for the human organism. In a work environment lit entirely by artificial light, it is important to ensure that the light sources are of varying intensity and color and that they are located in different parts of the room. It is a serious mistake to create a uniform lighting system consisting of fluorescent light fittings distributed evenly over the ceiling.

A special lighting design has been developed for the Himont and Enichem Elastomeri control rooms, using various kinds of light sources and different types of lighting (up lights, down lights, task lights, wall washers), the governing principle being variety, which is the fundamental characteristic of natural light. A large skylight in the ceiling creates the illusion of an opening onto the outside. Inside, the light sources vary. By such means, the aim was to produce visual stimuli capable of counteracting the immobility of electric light. During night shifts the level of illuminance increases to improve operator alertness. This "artificial skylight" has thus been optimized in the SIVRA laboratory and has been tested at the Lighting Research Center of Rensselaer Polytechnic Institute in Troy, NY with positive results.[52] (It is now produced in North America by Lite Control Corporation.) In order to lessen the contrast between exterior and interior, a provision was made for the installation of lights in the entrance corridor capable (by means of external sensors) of varying their intensity according to the degree of luminosity of natural light flowing in from outside. Subsequently, as one enters the control room and one's eyes adjust to the different light, the lighting level drops. In order to avoid reflection on the video screens and for the sake of the operators' comfort, the area around the control panel is lit by indirect light, and the surrounding surfaces and colors selected on the basis of their ability to absorb light.

The Plant Display Board In all control rooms and the head offices of industrial complexes, an overall picture of the layout of the plant is provided by brightly colored diagrams. A number of differently sized television screens provide pictures of various parts of the plant. At the control panel, the various production processes are visualized in computerized images that allow the operator to intervene by either pressing buttons or simply touching the screen. In the Enichem control room, the smooth white plaster of the entrance corridor becomes a roughly textured gray in the area surrounding the control panel and then changes again to leave naked reinforced concrete, lightly tinted with blue transparent paint. This sudden transition has its own special significance (as does the "crack" in the west wall that contains a clock), since it is here that the plant display board is placed. The large-scale representation of the plant hangs therefore on a bare wall of reinforced concrete. What this does is to signal, both spatially and formally, that representation and artifice are being used to maintain contact with reality and to enable people to act upon it more efficiently. This is, in fact, one of the principal problems of the "man–machine system" and people working with virtual realities (computers). There is always the danger that people end up retreating into the enclosed world of their own mind, becoming distracted, and losing contact with reality. After several hours in a completely closed and therefore hypostimulatory environment, the human brain enters a state of lethargy from which it cannot be roused simply by the flashing of lights on a control panel. In a windowless control room, dangerous situations may arise that catch the operator totally unaware and in a state of deep relaxation.

Furnishings   The rather special nature of the furnishings in the Himont control room is intended to dedramatize a potentially dangerous environment and counteract the feelings of fear and panic that such an environment can arouse. The furniture is arranged in such a way as to promote a good sense of direction. The command panel faces the north wall so that, even while there is no direct view of the plant, some form of contact with it is maintained.

(*Below left and right, and right*): The somewhat unusual form of the furnishings is meant to dedramatize a potentially dangerous environment and allay feelings of fear and panic that may arise in complex working situations. Himont control room, Ferrara, Italy, 1989. Design: Piera Scuri and Douglas Skene. (Photo: Dida Biggi.)

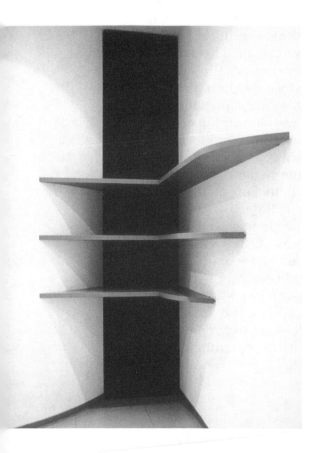

(*Right*): Exterior view, control room, Enichem Elastomeri, Ferrara, Italy, 1990. Architects: Piera Scuri and Douglas Skene. (Photo: Dida Biggi.)

The Exterior   The exterior of the control room also plays a very important role. Industrial complexes are often situated in somewhat unstructured spaces. A control room with a precise, clearly defined shape can become a very important point of reference within the plant. The problem is of a mental rather than aesthetic nature, in that a control room of this type helps individuals working inside it to form clear and well-organized mental maps.

ULYSSES' CHAINS

Space is not simply a container for work, but its tool, and is one of the factors that influence its quality, whether in a positive or negative sense. Indeed, space constitutes a source of stimuli and information that is intercepted by the perceptual apparatus and elaborated by the brain. Our actions are therefore, in part, responses to certain types of stimulation.

Highly technological environments are usually environments that have been planned for machines, and as a result, they are sensorially deficient as far as living organisms are concerned. In the first place, they are often constructed of synthetic materials. Plastic may be made to simulate any number of different materials, from wood to marble to metal, but only as far as appearance is concerned: It cannot deceive our sense of touch. One of the major defects of an environment made out of synthetic materials is its failure to stimulate our sense of touch—on the contrary, it anaesthetizes it. Not to mention the type of message that an environment of this type communicates at a cognitive or symbolic level. Failure to stimulate the senses (touch, sight, hearing, smell, etc.) means depriving the brain of basic tools for the establishment of good contact with reality. Numerous experiments

have been carried out on the effects of sensory deprivation: Above all else what happens is that individuals lose any notion of time, and the circadian rhythm becomes desynchronized. Studies of sensory perception and its influence on the central nervous system have been made by the Russian researchers Valentin Lebedev and Aleksei Leonov. In one experiment, they compared the different reactions of different individuals subjected to total sensory deprivation. The subjects (who were fitted with earplugs, dressed in special suits and gloves that cancelled out all sense of touch, and closed in a dark room) began after a certain time to experience hallucinations.[53] Other experiments conducted by Pavlov show that in order for the cerebral cortex to function properly, it has to be charged by a series of nervous impulses supplied by the sensory organs. When no such stimulus is forthcoming, the uniformity and monotony of impressions gained have the effect of reducing the level of energy (or tone) of the cerebral cortex. And this can easily lead to disorders in the psychic functions. The senses do not serve simply for the perception of the surroundings: They play a fundamental role in keeping our organism in contact with reality and "our feet on the ground." To anaesthetize (or deceive) the senses means in a certain sense to disconnect the brain (a similar thing happens in psychosis; only here the causes are of an endogenous type).

Considered thus, space is particularly important when it comes to planning control rooms or environments that are characterized anyway by a high level of artificiality and human interaction with advanced technologies used as a means of control. Within such spaces, it is necessary to introduce or at least recreate artificially (at least in part) the stimuli supplied by the natural environment in order to avoid the dangers described above. Interaction with advanced technologies essentially means to be immersed in a virtual dimension. Therefore, in addition to the preexistent problem of detachment from reality, there is also (and this is no coincidence) a lack of adequate sensory stimuli. It is difficult to work in an alert manner under such conditions (alertness means retaining the capacity to react quickly to reality). Planning environments in which individuals interact with advanced technolo-

gies essentially means tying ropes with which to bind Ulysses
to the mast while he listens to the sirens' song. Ulysses is
right: Their song is irresistible, but not worth risking one's
life for.

APPENDIX: LIGHT AS THERAPY

ALESSANDRO MELUZZI

Light and Biological Rhythms

The introduction of artificial light has greatly modified the parameter of man's exposure to sunlight over the last hundred years. During the course of this century, there has been a growing tendency to substitute natural light with artificial light, for the sake of convenience and with little regard as to the effect this might have on our health. Beneath such a process lies an implicit prejudice: Natural light is not indispensable to the psychophysical health of human beings.

Scientists working in space research have for some time been studying the body's reactions to living and working in enclosed, highly technological environments that are devoid of natural air and light. They have observed that the absence of natural light for long periods of time causes both psychological and physiological damage to the human body, with ailments ranging from detachment from reality (solipsistic syndrome), to depression, insomnia, worry, asthenia, hypotension, vitamin deficiency, desynchronization of the sleep-wake cycle, slowdown of the reflexes, bone decalcification, and weakening of the immune system.

Sunlight is thus essential for our health as a whole as well as for keeping the body in synchrony with the external environment and its periodic variations.

The importance of light as a synchronizer of our biological and psychological rhythms is also evident in the recent discovery of its effectiveness in treating certain types of depression (seasonal depression) and sleep disturbances. However, this applies only to light that reproduces natural sunlight, that is, light with a full spectrum wavelength and intensity of over 2500 lux.

The outcome of such studies seems to provide further confirmation of certain intuitions shared by philosophic-religious cultures of the past. One example of this is the greeting of the sun in oriental religion, during which the subject turns to face the sun and, in a sort of *ante litteram* light therapy, recites the mantra of thanks to light and the sun.

In sharp contrast to this style of life, with its intrinsic bond, or rather identification between man and nature, are the results of research conducted recently in California into the amount of exposure to sunlight undergone by people over 60. According to this study, in the sunny state of California, the elderly expose themselves to direct sunlight for less than 30 minutes each day. This confirms the importance of designing living environments in which the "light" factor is treated as a determining element for health in a confined microclimate.

The results of the most recent studies conducted into the relationship between human health and environment, show that the fundamental task to be undertaken in designing environments today is to contribute to repairing the fragile and damaged bond that unites man to the natural ecosystem of which he is a part.

The price to be paid for living in a space that deprives us of the natural elements that have shaped our body in the course of evolution is illness and the loss of our psychophysical homeostasis.

For many years, the medical sciences have studied human physiological phenomena and pathological processes without linking them to the ecological context in which man lived. Paradoxically, the relationship between living things and the ecosystem (i.e., the environment with which an individual interacts) has for years been the province of psychologists, ethologists, and philosophers and been ignored by doctors.

Ever since the french physiologist Claude Bernard propounded his concept of the "milieu interieur"—that is, the theory according to which the body tends to maintain over time a sort of homeostasis of all of its constituent parts—the possibility of any fluctuation in biological phenomena has been implicitly denied. In reality, the concept of homeostasis describes an active process of interdependence between a situation of balance and one of imbalance: In this context, ecological factors are not necessarily different from those affecting the homeostatic mechanisms, since the latter have also evolved in such a way as to allow the best possible adaptation of the body to the particular conditions of the environment in which it finds itself.

The time dimension was introduced to biology in the 1940s through the tenacity and perseverance of three scientists. Franz Halberg and his colleagues showed that, contrary to current opinion of the time, the number of leucocytes in peripheral blood is subject to considerable variations over a 24-hour period. In the same years, another scientist, J. Aschoff, who was working on the body's adaptation to cold, had noticed that human body temperature is subject to spontaneous and regular daily fluctuations that are independent of the temperature variations in the environment. But it was A. Reinberg, studying the daily variations of water and electrolytes in urinary excretions, who introduced to physiology the "biological cycle" concept as an event that repeats itself constantly in time. In Italy, the Ceresa and Angeli group pursued an advanced line of research into a new chronobiological outlook in endocrinology. It is precisely from the recognition of biological temporality and the intrinsic periodicity of living matter that cronobiology was born, propounding itself as an innovative scientific discipline based on the assumption that "biological rhythms"—that is, cyclical biological phenomena—do exist, with a definite and species—specific frequency that is apparent even in the absence of environmental stimuli. Moreover, chronobiology does not only give rise to concepts of a physiological (chronophysiological) order, but lays particular emphasis on pathological changes in rhythmic structure (chronopathology) and the timing of therapy (chronotherapy).

Chronobiology is a pioneering science as far as the study of the links between the internal and external ecosystem is concerned.

Light and its rhythm are the principal synchronizers of human and animal rhythms, both at the psychobiological and behavioral level.

The North American journal *Psychosomatic Medicine* recently published the results of a study carried out on a strictly statistical basis into the length of stay and the incidence of complications experienced by acute patients in intensive care wards; a comparison was made between subjects who were able to see a green space outside the window with subjects who could not. The result might seem all too obvious to some, but patients who had a view onto a brightly lit green space had a shorter stay in the hospital and presented fewer complications than those without.

There are after all, very ancient and profound reasons why the sight of a colored, brightly lit vista modulates our mental and physical mechanisms, the explanation for which may be found in the history of our species. Despite the fact that today we live our whole life under the effects of strong artificial light, our underlying biological rhythms are determined by the rhythms of natural light, which is to say, the cycle of days and nights and of the seasons (hormones, for instance, follow a 24-hour pattern).

In short, it is rather as if the internal ecosystem of our cells and physiology were obliged to keep pace with the rhythms of the external ecosystem, which in turn is determined by astronomical and climatic cycles.

When this equilibrium is destroyed or upset, we experience discomfort, then illness. There is one type of psychiatric disorder, named SAD by American researchers (i.e., seasonal affective disorder), that especially affects people living in closed environments in those areas of the world where the activating and synchronizing action of the sun is particularly weak during winter: This includes many parts of the United States, Canada, and Scandinavia, etc. A type of illness has been observed in these places that is characterized by depressive moods, lack of interest in sex, inhibition of movement and ideas, excessive fatigue, and a pathological "hunger" for sweet foods that results in obesity. Less acute forms of SAD are also found at other latitudes, however.

The importance of sunlight for the vital functions of all living things, from one-celled organisms to human beings, has long been recognized, but although the biological effects of light on plants are well known, its effects on the health and well-being of man are still unknown.

Knowledge gained in the last few years on this subject has shown the enormous importance of natural light in maintaining the biological balance. After food, light is the most important source of energy for the control of the life functions of every living thing.

The therapeutic effects of light in the treatment of certain common illnesses such as psoriasis, acne, and infant jaundice have been known for some time. Only recently has light been used in the treatment of all the forms of "desynchronization" mentioned above. The rationale for this came from recognizing the influence of light on the diencephalic structures, conditioning the secretion of hormones on the one hand and the variations in receptor sensitivity and, consequently, the functions of the neurotransmitter system on the other.

Already in the 1960s, research on animals in captivity had shown that light influences a large number of biological activities and functions, such as sexual development, reproduction, moulting, migration, the sleep-wake cycle, and the metabolism. Only recently, however, has light's effect on man and its influence in the psycho-neuro-endochrinal sphere been examined.

Clinical trials of phototherapy on patients with nonseasonal depression have recently been conducted by our research group, with remarkable results as far as the attenuation of depressive symptoms was concerned.[54] Of the 19 subjects who underwent a 10-day course of phototherapy, a significant

SUMMARY OF PSYCHOMETRIC EVALUATION (1)

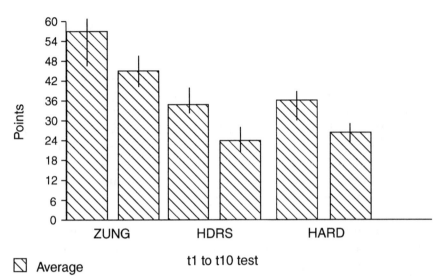

☒ Average

t1 to t10 test

Psychometric evaluation of 19 patients (non-seasonal depressives) treated with photo-therapy for 10 consecutive days. In the tests for depression (Zung, HDRS, and HARD), there was a significant point reduction at +10.

improvement of depressive symptoms was seen in 14 of these, that is, 73 percent.

Moreover, a Student "t-test" was carried out comparing the data, and this confirmed—at least in regard to the tests on depression—the importance of the results from a statistical point of view as well.

Positive results regarding depressive symptoms emerged from both the self-evaluation questionnaire (Zung), as well as individual tests (HDRS and HARD), thus showing clearly that there had been a reduction of both subjective and objective symptoms.

The self-evaluation tests for anxiety also resulted, in most cases, in a reduction of points following phototherapy treatment. This change is owed in our opinion to the individual's state of mind at that moment and the way this influences his self-image and way of life. Positive reaction to therapy in 73 percent of cases is a most satisfactory result, bearing in mind the seriousness of depressive illness, the necessity of a rapid and effective treatment (positive response to phototherapy was apparent as early as the third or fourth day of treatment) in patients who often did not show any significant improvement with antidepressant drug therapy.

Furthermore, in another study conducted by our research group, it was revealed that as well as reducing depressive symptoms in depressed patients, phototherapy also brings about a change in the circadian rhythmic activity of the monoamine oxidase in blood platelets. The circadian rhythm of blood platelet monoamine oxidase in depressives differs in fact from that of healthy individuals; treatment with phototherapy brings the circadian curve of monamine oxidase activity in depressed subjects into line with that of healthy control subjects.[55]

In men and animals, variations in light intensity are registered, via the retina, by an organ called the pineal gland. The sensitivity of the pineal gland varies from species to species: In the rat, melatonin production is suppressed by a light intensity of .0005 µW/centimeters,[56] whereas in man, at least 150 µW/centimeters is needed to do this.[57] The human pineal gland differs quantitively rather than qualitatively from that of laboratory animals in its response to light: Perhaps man, in adapting to artificial light, has remained sensitive only to the natural cycle of light and darkness. Exposure at night to 2500 lux can quickly suppress melatonin levels; a 50 percent reduction is obtained with 1500 lux, suggesting that there is a direct link between light intensity and hormone excretion.[58]

In considering the biological effects of light on rhythmical activities, the light referred to is natural sunlight. Conventional lightbulbs reproduce only a part of the wavelength of natural light and are chromatically unbalanced, thus depriving man of the biological benefits of full spectrum natural light. Sunlight consists of a wide spectrum of wavelength and colors, although some of these are filtered out by the atmosphere. The spectrum of visible light is responsible for the effects on the mesencephalic structures and consequently also the chronobiological program.

DAYLIGHT

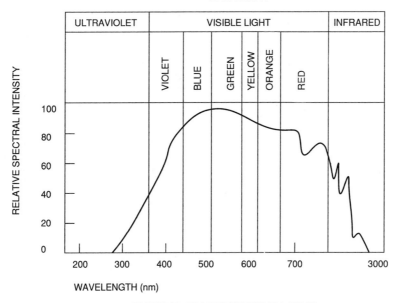

TYPICAL FLUORESCENT LIGHT

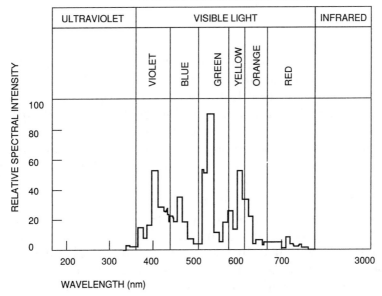

Three graphs indicating the average amount of energy emitted by the light source in question. The curves of the tungsten and neon lightbulbs show how limited their spectrums are (in terms of quantity and type of energy) in comparison with solar light.

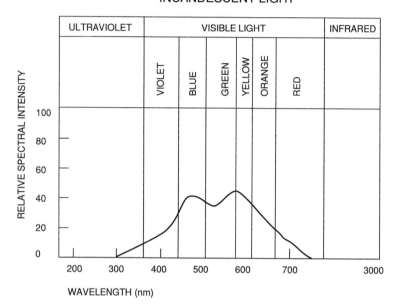

The demands of work mean that human beings spend most of their time inside buildings, completely isolated from the influence of natural light. Offices, schools, hospitals, etc. are illuminated by a spectrally limited light; spending long periods, sometimes whole seasons, inside such places means that humans are deprived of the principal synchronizing factor of their circadian rhythm, with the result that they desynchronize.

Phototherapy is used to "shift" irregular biological rhythms back into phase, in what is therefore a "chronologizing" biological mechanism. We believe, however, that another way in which light exercises its biological influence is through a modulation of the psycho-neuro-endocrino-immunitary network, without necessarily resynchronizing it.

The parameters for judging the chronobiological activity of light (in addition, as we have repeatedly said, to full spectrum) are as follows.

Conditions for the Administering of Phototherapy

Light intensity: 2000/2500 lux
Wavelength: 509 nanometers
Length of exposure: from 40 minutes up to 3 hours per day
Time of exposure: early hours of morning
Length of treatment: 7 to 10 days
Distance from light source: 70 to 150 centimeters
Position of patient: seated, supine

Intensity   This is measured as the brightness or quantity of the light directed at the patient. Patients respond to an intensity of 2000/2500 lux, which is the amount needed to suppress nocturnal secretion of melatonin in man.[59]

Wavelength   The most effective wavelengths seem to be those around 509 nanometers.[60]

Length of Exposure   Patient response seems to be proportional to the length of treatment although this varies considerably from individual to individual, in that each seems to have a personal threshold. From one to three hours of treatment per day is generally held to be necessary.[61]

Time of Exposure   The importance of the time at which exposure takes place is still being discussed. At first, phototherapy concentrated on extending the photoperiod, administering light at dawn and dusk for a total of about six hours.[62]

It has been observed[63] that in addition to its antidepressive effect, morning light brings forward melatonin production, whereas evening light delays it. Experiments were therefore performed in which subjects were exposed to either morning or evening light, the aim being to bring forward or delay the circadian rhythms.

Several studies[64] show that the circadian rhythms are more sensitive to the influence of light in the first hours of the morning. In fact, only half an hour's exposure to early morning light brought about an improvement in symptoms.[65]

During phototherapy, the patient is placed about 70 centimeters from the light source and is free to indulge in any kind of activity he or she chooses (reading, eating, knitting, etc.) on the condition that every five minutes, the patient turns his or her eyes toward the light for at least one minute.

The literature is concordant in the observation that patients begin to respond to therapy after two to four days, whereas relapses may occur days or weeks after the suspension of treatment.[66]

In looking at the positive therapeutic results obtained by phototherapy, its significant placebo component must be considered: The symbolic significance of light and patients' expectations of a nonpharmacological approach should both be taken into account. Some studies have been conducted with this factor in mind. In 1988, Kripke and his colleagues carried out a preliminary study on 12 depressed patients who were exposed on alternate days, for a period of one hour, to a brilliant white light or weak red light. The results confirmed the therapeutic action of the former.

As well as confirmation of this type, some considerations may also be made in favor of the generality of the placebo component:[67]

> The improvement of 75 percent of patients treated, which agrees with data in the literature, is very high.
>
> The therapeutic effects may be reproduced in different places and the same patients at different times.
>
> The symptoms reappear following suspension or interruption of treatment.

Side effects appear mostly in the first days of treatment and consist of violent headache, nausea, and irritation of the eyes, generally disappearing within a few days. The potential toxicity of the UV band should be borne in mind, however, especially in chronic therapies. In such cases, it is preferable to use light sources that do not have a UV band; their effectiveness as therapy or in prevention is comparable to that of full spectrum lightbulbs.

To sum up, phototherapy may at present be considered to represent a valid therapeutic approach for desynchronization disorders, although some aspects have yet to be clarified. The positive effects of this treatment are of undisputed practical significance: It is not a pharmaceutical therapy, it does not give rise to intolerance, and there are hardly any side effects.

The effectiveness of phototherapy in treating SAD is confirmed by data recorded in the large body of literature published over the last 10 years, the results of which have been unequivocal. However, the small number of patients treated, contradictory nature of certain pathogenetic mechanisms, and methodological difficulties that are related to the obvious impossibility of conducting double blind studies mean that, as a treatment, phototherapy is still at an experimental stage.

Recently, phototherapy was proposed by various authors as a method of treating several illnesses in which the time factor played a part. For example, it was shown that alcohol abuse has a cyclical progression, with peaks in the autumn months (October and November). Alcoholism is, of course, a multidimensional problem and should be treated as such; in this perspective, phototherapy should be used to complete the therapeutic strategy.[68]

In the United States and former Soviet Union, it has been suggested that wide-spectrum light be used in spaceships as a biorhythmical body regulator and way of safeguarding astronauts from potentially hazardous environmental stimuli.[69]

The range of situations for which this therapy could be used is, however, enormous, if one contemplates the number of disorders characterized by the biorhythm being upset: jet lag, insomnia especially in the elderly whose sleep-wake cycle is upset, psychosomatic disorders linked to shift work, or certain types of cephalea.

Summary of Possible Uses for Phototherapy

Shift work disorders
Jet lag
Cephalea
Seasonal Affective Disorders (SAD)

Eating disorders
Sleeping disorders (insomnia and hypersomnia)
Synchronization of drug therapy
Permanence in space
Alcoholism

ENDNOTES

Chapter 1: Artificial Versus Natural

1. Prak, N. (1975), *The Visual Perception of the Built Environment,* Delft, Delft University Press, p. 47.
2. Starobinski, J. (1964), *L'invention de la liberté,* Geneva, Skira, p. 15. Praz, M. (1981), *La filosofia dell'arredamento,* Milan, Longanesi, pp. 22–23.
3. Machado, P. (1989), "Human ecological approach," in *Building Evaluation,* New York, Plenum Press.
4. Goethe, J.W. (1989), La teoria dei colori, Milan, il saggiatore.
5. Castelli, C. (ed.) (1976), *Colordinamo 1976,* Milan, Laboratorio di Micerca Montefibre (special edition).
6. Johnson D.R. & Holbrow Ch., eds., (1977), *Space Settlements, A Design Study*, NASA SP-413, Washington D.C., NASA Scientific and Technical Information Office, p. 29.
7. The excerpt by Le Camus de Mezières is from Starobinski, *op. cit.,* pp. 56–57. On the importance of simulation see also: Simon, H.A. (1969), *The Sciences of the Artificial,* Cambridge, the MIT Press, p. 18.

Chapter 2: Isolated and Confined Environments

8. Leonov, A. and Lebedev, V. (1968), *Perception of Space and Time in Outer Space,* Moscow, Navka Press, p. 5 (translated as NASA 4-5-1968).

9. For example, at the University of Wisconsin, the School of Architecture and Urban Planning offers courses in space architecture under the direction of Professor Gary Moore.

10. Aquarius is a NASA marine laboratory at Salt River Canyon, St. Croix, Caribbean Sea, about 4000 meters below sea level.

11. See Carmody, J. (1992), *Design of Underground Environments,* New York, Van Nostrand Reinhold.

12. Wise J.A., ed. (1983), *The Human Factors of Underground Work Environments*, Technical Report, Department of Architecture, University of Washington, Seattle. Gerber, J. (1986), *Preliminary Analysis of Human Factors, Study of an Analagous Environment: Submarines.* ESA D/SSP-LTPO (86)1. Zrudio, L. (1970), *Psychological Problems and Environmental Design in the North,* Quebec, Université Laval. Hughey J. and Tye, R. (1984), "Psychological reactions working underground: A study of attitudes, beliefs and evaluations," in *Underground Space.* New York, Pergamon Press, pp. 381–386.

13. Oil platform workers, especially those working on platforms in the Arctic seas, may work shifts of about 15 days. Shifts are generally organized on a 60-day basis, with 30 days being spent on the platform and 30 on the mainland. Obviously, the number of people that can be on a platform at any one time varies: from 30 to 100 up to about 200 on the North Sea platforms.

14. Norman, J.N. (1988), *Systems of Health Care in Analagous Situations Offshore/North Sea and Antarctica.* Aberdeen, U.K.: British Antarctic Survey, Medical Unit, RGIT Survival Centre. A comparative study has been carried out using a database of the 2000 accidents that have taken place in the British Antarctic territories among different population groups over a period of 25 years. There were numerous parallels, the most remarkable of which was the high incidence of gastrointestinal disorders and the low incidence of cardiovascular problems.

Chapter 3: Space Perception as a Design Parameter

15. Zevi, B. (1973), *Il linguaggio moderno dell'architettura* Turin,

Einaudi, pp. 146–148 (the passages in quotes are taken from E.T. Hall, *The Hidden Dimension*).

16. Sechenov, I.M. (1952), *Izbrannye proizvedeniya (Selected Works)*, Vol. 1, Moscow, Izdat. Akad. Nauk. S.S.S.R. Cited in Leonov, A. and Lebedev, V. (1968), *Perception of Space and Time in Outer Space*, Moscow, Navka Press, p. 17 (translated as NASA 4-5-1968).

17. Leonov, A. and Lebedev, V. (1968), *Perception of Space and Time in Outer Space*, Moscow, Navka Press, p. 13 (translated as NASA 4-5-1968).

18. Leonov and Lebedev, *op. cit.*, p. 15.

19. Leonov and Lebedev, *op. cit.*, p. 17.

20. Leonov and Lebedev, *op. cit.*, p. 41.

21. Leonov and Lebedev, *op. cit.*, p. 19.

22. Leonov and Lebedev, *op. cit.*, p. 21.

23. Proshansky, H. et al. (1983), "Place identity: Physical world socialization of the self," in *Journal of Environmental Psychology*, Vol. 3, pp. 57–83. Coles, R. (1970), *Uprooted Children*, Pittsburgh, Penn., Pittsburgh University Press. Spielberger, C. (ed.) (1979), *Stress and Anxiety*, Vol. 6, Washington, D.C., Hemisphere Publishing Co.

24. Ittelson, W. (ed.) (1973), *Environment and Cognition*, New York, Seminar Press.

25. Barker, R. (1968), *Ecological Psychology*, Stanford, Calif., Stanford University.

26. Hall, E.T. (1966), *The Hidden Dimension*, New York, Doubleday-Anchor Press, p. 83.

27. Hall, E.T. (1959), *The Silent Language*, New York, Anchor Books, p. 179.

28. Leonov and Lebedev, *op. cit.*, p. 21.

29. Zevi, B. (1973), *Il linguaggio moderno dell'architettura*, Turin, Einaudi, *passim*.

30. Zevi, B., *op. cit.*, p. 62.

Chapter 4: The Perception of Light and Color

31. Hyman, J.W. (1990), *The Light Book*, New York, St. Martin's Press, p. 23.

32. Meluzzi, A. et al. (1990), *La luce come terapia*, Pavia, Edizioni Mediche Italiane, p. 34.

33. Boyce, P. (1981), *Human Factors in Lighting,* London, Applied Science Publishers, p. 334.

34. Kraus, R.F. and Buffler, P.A. (1979), "Sociocultural stress and the American native in Alaska: An analysis of changing patterns of psychiatric illness and alcohol abuse among Alaskan natives," in *Culture, Medicine and Psychiatry,* Vol. 3, pp. 111–151.

35. It is not known exactly why exposure to bright light has a positive effect on mood. There are numerous theories. One suggests thought that it suppresses the secretion of melatonin, a photosensitive hormone produced by the pineal gland; another theory is that it affects the serotoninergic system (serotonin, the biochemical precursor of melatonin, plays an important role in the control of numerous functions such as mood, sleep, body temperature, sexual behavior). (See Meluzzi et al., *op. cit.,* pp. 85–87.)

36. The soprachiasmatic nuclei are probably not the only pacemakers; see Hyman, *op. cit.,* p. 13. Melatonin is involved in the regulation of the sleep-wake cycle: Taken in moderate doses, it induces sleep. It is also given to blind people with desynchronization problems. Meluzzi et al., *op. cit.,* p. 37.

37. De Maio fed diurnal animals during the night. After some time the animals changed—desynchronized—their circadian parameters such as body temperature (see Meluzzi et al., *op. cit.,* p. 13). The same results were obtained in experiments with monkeys confined for a year to environments lit wholly by artificial light [see Leonov and Lebedev (1968), *op. cit.,* Moscow, Navka Press, (translated as NASA 4-5-1968, p. 92)].

38. In a paper presented to the International Convention on Space, "Città e cittadini dello Spazio," held at CNR headquarters in Rome in March 1991.

39. Meluzzi et al., *op. cit.,* p. 37.

40. Boyce, *op. cit.,* p. 334.

41. Thornton, W.A. (1972), "Colour discrimination index," in *Journal of Optical Society of America,* Vol. 62, p. 191.

42. Goethe, *op. cit.,* p. 166.

43. Wise, J. (1988), *The Human Factors of Color in Environmental Design: A Critical Review,* NASA Grant No. NCC 2-4041.

44. Gerard, R.M. (1958), *Differential Effects of Colored Lights on Psychophysiological Functions,* Los Angeles, Calif., UCLA, Ph.D. dissertation.

45. Itten, J. (1961), *Kunst der farbe,* Ravensburg, Otto Mayer Verlag.

46. Kwallek, N. (1992), *Interior Space for Outer Space: Impact of Color on Crew Satisfaction and Productivity,* paper presented to 1st International Conference on Design for Extreme Environments, Houston, Texas, Assembly University, Nov. 12–15, 1991.

47. One might recall in this context the various experiments carried out in the 1980s on the uses of color in order to engender certain feelings (according to Goethe, color has a much more powerful effect when it is on walls, i.e., when it surrounds us, than when it is confined to objects). One such example is the design of the living quarters for the space station MIR, which caused quite a sensation. The rest and work zones were painted in different colors—green and yellow, respectively—and a special lighting system was designed. These modifications were made after previous astronauts developed a series of psychophysiological problems. In the former Tombs correctional facility in Manhattan, Professor Richard Wener and his team conducted a study of the effects of color and certain spatial configurations on the behavior of inmates. Gary Winkel, Professor at the City University in New York, has carried out numerous experiments on the influence of light and color on human behavior. The best known of these is his study (made in the mid–1980s) for the emergency ward of Bellevue Hospital in New York. The success of the experiment allowed him to continue his work in several museums and airports in America. His interest centered on the role color and light can play in helping people find their bearings in buildings that have a complex layout and are psychologically stressful, as well as their potential influence at a therapeutic level. See Winkel, Gary (1985), *The Environmental Psychology of the Hospital: Is the Cure Worse than the Illness?,* New York, The Haworth Press.

48. Goethe, *op. cit.,* p. XVII.

49. Boyce, *op. cit.,* pp. 168–174.

Chapter 5: Design of Windowless Environments

50. The laboratory is situated near Guzzini Illuminazione srl Industries at Recanati in central Italy. The Lighting Research Center of the Rensselaer Polytechnic Institute of Troy, New York took part in the project. The American team is made up of

Professor Peter Boyce, who works on problems concerning light and human factors, and Dr. Mark Rea, the director of the Lighting Research Center. The laboratory was designed by Piera Scuri, Douglas Skene, and Daniele Bedini. Others involved in the SIVRA project are Pier Giovanni Ceregioli, Franco Nibaldi, and Pasquale Cosenza of Guzzini Illuminazione. The laboratory was built in collaboration with the following companies: Sadi, Oece, Unifor, Bardelli, Limonta.

51. Taylor, J.J. (1985), "R&D status report nuclear power division," in *Electric Power Research Institute Journal,* July/Aug., p. 64. Leckner, J.M. (1989), "Research helps EdF improve operating practices and control rooms," in *Nuclear Engineering International,* Nov., pp. 38–39. Jansen, J.P. (1984), "The control room of the future," *The Chemical Engineer,* March, pp. 22–25.

52. Boyer, P.R., Beckstead, J.W., Eklund, N.U., Strobel, R.W., and Rea, M.S. *Lighting the graveyard shift: The influence of a Day-light-simulating skylight on the task performance and mood of night shift workers,* Lighting Research Center, Rensselaer Polytechnic Institute, Troy, NY, 1993.

53. Leonov and Lebedev, *op. cit.,* p. 73.

54. This study to be published.

55. Meluzzi, A. et al. (1990), *op. cit.*

56. Webb, S. et al. (1985), "Photoreceptor damage and eye pigmentation: Influence on the sensitivity of rat pineal activity and melatonin levels to light at night," in *Neuroendocrinology,* No. 40, p. 205.

57. Reiter, N.J. (1986), "Pineal melatonin production: Photoperiodic and hormonal influences," in *Advances in Pineal Research,* No. 1, p. 17.

58. Lewy, A.J. et al. (1980), "Light suppresses melatonin secretion in humans," in *Science,* No. 210, p. 1267.

59. Lewy, A.J. et al. (1982), "Bright artificial light treatment of manic-depressive patient with seasonal mood cycle," in *American Journal of Psychiatry,* No. 139, p. 1496.

60. Brainard, G.C. et al. (1985), "Effects of light wavelengths on the suppression of nocturnal plasma melatonin in normal volunteers," in *Annals New York Academy of Science,* No. 15, p. 571.

61. Lewy, A.J. and Sack,R.L. (1987), "Phase typing and bright light therapy of cronobiologic sleep and mood disorders," in Halaris,

A., *Chronobiology and Psychiatric Disorders,* New York, Elsevier.

62. Rosenthal, N.E. et al. (1985), "Seasonal affective disorder," in *Archives of General Psychiatry,* No. 41, p. 72.

63. Czeisler, C.A. et al. (1986), "Bright light resets the human circadian pacemaker independent of the timing of the sleep-wake cycle," in *Science,* No. 237, p. 667.

64. Lewy, A.J. et al. (1986), "Immediate and delayed effects of bright light on human melatonin production: Shifting 'dawn' and 'dusk' shift the dim light melatonin onset," in *Annals New York Academy of Science,* No. 453, p. 235.

65. Kripke, D.F. et al. (1983), "Bright white light alleviates depression," in *Psychiatry Research,* No. 10, p. 105.

66. Wirz-Justice, A. (1986), "Light therapy of depression: Present status, problems and perspectives," in *Psychopathology,* No. 19, p. 136.

67. *Ibid.*

68. Hyman, J. (1990), *The Light Book,* Los Angeles, Calif., Jeremy P. Tarcher, Inc., p. 181.

69. Coleman, R. (1986), *Wide Awake at 3:00 a.m.: By Choice or by Chance?,* New York, W.H. Freeman and Co.